Your Wild and Precious Life

On grief, hope and rebellion

LIZ JENSEN

CANONGATE

This paperback edition published in 2025 by Canongate Books

First published in Great Britain in 2024 by Canongate Books Ltd,
14 High Street, Edinburgh EH1 1TE

canongate.co.uk

1

For permission credits, please see p. 219

British Library Cataloguing-in-Publication Data
A catalogue record for this book is available on
request from the British Library

ISBN 978 1 83726 022 5

Typeset in Bembo by Palimpsest Book Production Ltd,
Falkirk, Stirlingshire

Printed and bound by CPI Group (UK) Ltd, Croydon CR0 4YY

Liz Jensen is the author of eight acclaimed novels including *The Ninth Life of Louis Drax* and the climate thrillers *The Rapture* and *The Uninvited*. She is a founder of the ecological campaign group Writers Rebel and the creator of the Rebel Library. She lives in Copenhagen.

@LizJensenWriter | lizjensen.com

Raphaël Coleman was a wildlife biologist and activist. He worked with wildlife sanctuaries all over the world, created the international wildlife workers' network The Wildwork and campaigned with Extinction Rebellion under the alias Iggy Fox. He died suddenly in February 2020 at the age of twenty-five.

IggyFox.com

'Like nothing else I've ever read. Uplifting, sublimely beautiful, funny, skilful, courageous and deeply necessary, *Your Wild and Precious Life* is a luminous love letter to a lost son, a spiritual journey and a celebration of the living world in all its astonishing manifestations'
LALINE PAULL

'A mother's unflinching account of finding meaning in her son's unexpected death. His is not the only death to haunt the pages of this raw and urgent memoir. Jensen's focus shifts between her own grief, and a mourning for lost nature'
GUARDIAN

'Heartbreaking yet compulsively readable. A call to action over the most pressing global issue that confronts human survival'
LOUISE DOUGHTY

'A deeply moving, powerful, resonant book about the enormity of love and grief, and what it is to be alive yet mortal'
RACHEL CLARKE

'Written with power and emotion, [this] beautiful and moving book explores how we live, love and grieve'
STYLIST

'Profoundly moving and inspiring. For a book about grief, it is dazzlingly life affirming and energising. I read it in one sitting'
ESTHER FREUD

'Devastating, luminous and gloriously alive. The presence – rather than absence – of Liz's son exalts every landscape, inner and outer, his spirit felt so deeply that at times he seems to co-author the prose'
CHLOE ARIDJIS

'This book is made of diamonds and tears, glittering with brilliance, a work of priceless insight'
JAY GRIFFITHS

For all the brave defenders of this wild and precious world, and in loving memory of Raphaël Coleman, 1994–2020

Who would have thought my shrivel'd heart
Could have recover'd greennesse? It was gone
      Quite under ground; as flow'rs depart
To see their mother-root, when they have blown,
         Where they together
         All the hard weather
Dead to the world, keep house unknown.
         From 'The Flower', George Herbert

Your body is away from me
but there is a window open
from my heart to yours.
From this window, like the moon
I keep sending news secretly.

         Rumi

Another world is not only possible, she is on
her way. On a quiet day, I can hear her breathing.
         Arundhati Roy

CONTENTS

PROLOGUE

Every parent fears losing a child, but when my first son was born I was gripped with an unshakable terror that it would happen to me. Dismissing it wasn't an option: its hold was too firm. It made me feel lonely and furtive and ashamed, the way awful secrets do. I couldn't tell anybody, because if I said it aloud it might come true. But finally, when I became pregnant for the second time, I cracked.

I'm going to lose a child, I told the therapist. I don't know which one. But one of them will die.

He took my distress seriously. My fear was symptomatic of magical thinking, he said – the form of superstition that convinces you of non-existent realities or connections. But that didn't make ignoring it an option. Instead, I had to examine where it came from and take active steps to dissolve its power. So after investigating it over several weeks, I went on a small pilgrimage to make peace with something in my past. Placebo or not, the intervention worked: the curse, whether real or imaginary, was lifted. My second son was born, and as he and his brother grew up the old terror – *irrational fears of a young mother, 1989–1994* – lay half-forgotten in the mental equivalent of the kitchen drawer, along with pencils, used batteries and padlock keys.

And then the phone call came.

My younger son Raphaël had collapsed and died. It was inexplicable. He was twenty-five. In that moment, everything else collapsed and died too. My life. My world. My sense of meaning. And time itself.

When the ancient Greeks walked the earth there were two words for time: *chronos* and *kairos*. Chronos refers to the epochs, centuries, years, seasons, weeks, months and days, and their myriad subdivisions: it is what marks calendars, clocks and schedules, charting the forward movement of history and human lifetimes. But kairos embodies another kind of time altogether: the kind that disrupts chronology, foreclosing the future we reckoned on and forcing radical change. Kairos moments seem to come out of the blue. But nothing really does. Every life-changing moment has an invisible gestation. When the most likely cause of Raphaël's death emerged, it came with a name:

arrhythmogenic right ventricular dysplasia. The potential for a fatal electrical malfunction of his heart had been latent all along, quietly preparing for the catastrophe I had once intuited and then suppressed.

His death was my kairos moment. It catapulted me into a new dimension in which time, space and language ceased to function. Several times a day I'd say, aloud, 'Raph's dead', as if to understand the depth and permanence of it. I couldn't. But I kept saying it, like a terrible new mantra. What more was there to say?

But then, in traumatised, sporadic bursts, more words came: journal entries, letters, fragments, notes and semi-imagined conversations with the loving, talkative, argumentative, comical, visionary, stubborn, energetic, generous, eccentric young man who was – and still is – my child. They tumbled out chaotically, and they were as raw as I felt: as tortured, as hopeless and as confused.

If grief is the price of love, then when what we love vanishes, we pay it with a misery that approaches madness. But no feeling, however deep, is permanent. When kairos struck, breaking the invisible line I once thought of as natural progression and throwing me into a state of mental chaos like nothing I had ever known, I was forced to trust the constancy of change itself, and to surrender to all that rolled through me.

It's said that for grief to begin its work we must live

through it in every season. And sure enough, as spring turned to summer, then autumn and winter, I began to feel flickers of wonder, surprise, gratitude, even something close to joy. But kairos' most transcendent gift is still unfolding: a new way of inhabiting the world.

An acquaintance who lost a son said to me, soon after Raphaël's death: 'You get through it, but you never get over it.' I've come to believe that this wisdom applies not just to the grief of bereaved parents, but to the grief – past, present and anticipatory – of a civilisation in the midst of a rolling existential crisis, the full scope of which we can only guess at. Each passing year distorts the future we once expected. We're no longer who we were and we're not headed where we thought. To navigate the currents of this era of unprecedented turbulence, we will need to be imaginative, inventive and practical. And I believe we can be.

Today, every child is born into a rapidly vanishing Eden. As a wildlife biologist and environmental activist, Raphaël felt this viscerally. He could have sunk into apathy or depression in the face of the ecological desecration he saw every day. 'Every time I write about an endangered species, it feels like I'm writing its obituary,' he told me once. It grieved him, but it didn't deter him. His talent was to look for the tiny aperture at the heart of every crisis that lets the light in. When he found it, he did all he could to widen it, let in more light, help it spread. 'To some, collapse seems inevitable,' he wrote. 'To others, ambitious systemic change is not only necessary, but also offers an opportunity for hope.'

I tried to apply this to my own apocalypse. As I searched for new stories, rituals, knowledge and physical practices to alleviate my devastation and to simply stay alive, Raphaël and I began fresh conversations about the world. Weird, sometimes. Funny, often. Consoling, always. And riding the ever-changing waves of grief, I learned to heed the instincts that the process of civilisation has suppressed in our species: the instincts of the animal we are. In honouring my own creaturehood, and attending to my intimations of the numinous, I discovered strength within deepest pain.

I am not the same person I was before. After trauma, no one is. We hear about post-traumatic stress. But we hear less about post-traumatic growth, post-traumatic regeneration and post-traumatic spiritual awakening. Yet I have felt all these things, in my mind and my blood, and I inhabit my skin differently. I am less an 'I' and more a 'we'. This doesn't make me feel small. Instead, it frames me as a cell that pulses within the living body of a vast organism that is vital to my own survival and the survival of all that it contains.

My son's death will never make sense to me. But it has

taught me that it's possible to find other kinds of meaning, collectively and individually, in the loss of what we love. And in finding them, transform. Resilience is a seed that we all bear inside us. It germinates in emergencies. It sprouts whether we ask it to or not. It sets down roots in astonishing and unexpected ways. And if we notice it, and tend to it, it blooms. I have seen it among others who are bereaved. We are sadder than we were. But we cherish life more, because of all we owe it.

We have learned that if we love the world again, it will love us back.

PART ONE: OUT OF TIME

CHAPTER I: WILL YOU SURVIVE?

He is small, no older than seven.

I'm at the kitchen cooker making porridge, or maybe scrambling eggs. Something mummy-ish, I like to think – though the truth is I can't remember. But I remember that it's sunny outside, and the window's open, and the jasmine is blooming, and the scent is wafting in.

He appears before me barefoot in his stripy blue pyjamas. His default look is serious.

He says, 'I had a dream.' His voice is deeper than most children's, which gives everything he says a comical gravitas.

'What happened in it?'

'I had a disease and was going to die.'

I stop whatever I am doing. A cold ribbon of terror slides down my spine.

'Were you frightened?' I ask.

'No. But I had to tell you and Papa I was going to die. And when I did, you both went crazy. I said it was OK. I didn't mind dying. I wasn't scared or anything. But you kept crying and crying. I tried to make you stop. But I couldn't. I couldn't make you understand.'

Tears well in his astonishingly blue eyes. The dream has upset him – but the upsetting part is not his own death: it's his inability to stop our pain.

This is not the kind of dream that a mother who has already intuited a tragedy can forget. But it's the kind of dream she can suppress. And she knows how to suppress the unthinkable because she has done it before.

That cold winter day, I was in an apartment in Texas with a paper map of the Gulf Coast, highlighting the local flood zones for a story I was working on. A small succulent pot plant stood on the table. On my arrival the day before, I'd instinctively given it a quick squeeze to check whether it was plastic, because that's how realistic they are: you have to touch them – sniff them, perhaps lick them even – to tell. I'd occasionally felt tempted to buy one because they're plausible, decorative and no-maintenance. If I owned one, I wouldn't feel like a nurturer but nor would I feel that I'd failed at nurturing. I squeezed it again. It was plastic.

The news was showing Australian forests alive with scarlet flame, rolling smoke clouds, scorched koalas, birds with their wings on fire, and hillsides alive with panicked kangaroos. The next item was about the virus spreading from China, but I switched it off because I'd been feeling particularly good and I wanted to stay that way. It was a cold afternoon in early February, and I had five days ahead of me. I'd come from Los Angeles, where the boys' step-father Carsten and I were based while he was teaching. My rented apartment was clean, with understated furnishings, pale Venetian blinds and uniformly-white walls. If I squinted, I could be back home in Denmark.

I was putting the map in my rucksack, ready to go exploring, when my phone rang.

'Liz. It's Michel.' Michel is the father of my sons. We'd been divorced for twenty years and had had little contact since the boys grew up. But now there he was, on my phone. Crying.

'Is everything OK?' I asked. But I knew it couldn't be. Knew, immediately, what must have happened.

I thought: Which boy?

'It's Raphaël. Raphaël is dead.'

The word you reach for is the same in any language. *No. No. No. No.* Such a simple word. Denial, refusal.

Powerlessness. At first it was all I could say — as if rejecting the news with enough force would make it un-happen. *No.*

Raphaël was in South Africa because he planned to make a documentary about the Black Mambas and the Akashingas, the all-female anti-poaching units in South Africa and Zimbabwe. He'd signed up to the same gruelling, SAS-style anti-poaching course the women went on, so he could keep up when he filmed them on patrol. It was summer there, and he was due to stay for four months. He'd been there just four days.

'He collapsed.' Michel choked through his tears. 'I was in a taxi when I got the call. He was out on a training run. One minute he was with the others. He was running and singing. He was happy. Then he fell. And they couldn't . . . they couldn't . . .'

He broke off.

Running. Singing. Happy. Dead.

I sat there, numb.

When words finally emerged from me, I delivered them with absolute conviction, though I had no sense of where this conviction came from.

'This was going to happen. He was going to die, no matter what.'

It was as though another alien version of myself was speaking, from a place beyond my reach.

After we hung up, I wondered why I hadn't sensed the moment of his death. Why didn't it hit me like a telepathic gut-punch, the moment he left the world? I should have felt it coming, too: felt it the same way creatures sense the tiny pre-tremors of an earthquake. A bristling scruff, an electric pulse of blood, a hammering thorax. Something. *Then I could have warned him.* But there was nothing. Outside, the Houston light was steady and bright, and the Venetian blinds striped the wooden floor with sunshine. It was the kind of winter day that makes you glad to be alive. I didn't want to be alive. I wanted to be dead. But Raphaël – whatever was left of him – needed his family. We had to get to where he was, and be with him. Through tearful phone calls, Michel, our older son Matti and I agreed to meet in Johannesburg as soon as we could. Beyond that there was no plan. Through more tearful phone calls, I broke the news to Carsten, my brother and my stepdaughters, and booked a flight.

By the airport gate I ordered a large glass of Shiraz. When the barman handed it to me I took a big swig, then fumbled and dropped the glass. It smashed, spilling dark wine across the counter.

'I'm sorry,' I said as the barman mopped it up. 'My son just died.'

He looked up, stricken. Wordlessly, he poured me another glass.

'His name is Raphaël,' I told him. 'I have two sons, Matti and Raphaël. Raph's the younger one. He's a wildlife activist. He's also called Iggy Fox. Iggy's short for Icarus because he loves the Greek myths.'

The barman's eyes went dark with pain. As the wine began its important work, I asked him if he had kids too. Three, he told me. He gave more information about them but nothing stuck. My brain couldn't process anything in the normal way. My healthy son had inexplicably dropped dead and everything – even basic conversation – felt alien. I kept drinking. I'd asked him about his children because I wanted him to imagine one of them dying too. I needed another human being to imagine this with me. But he couldn't. He couldn't imagine it. Nor could I. Even though I'd just lost one. *Especially* because I'd just lost one. I'd lived with the fear of it without ever picturing how it would feel. Now I knew.

I drank the rest of my wine, then got up to leave. 'Please,' I said. 'Is it OK for you to give me a hug?'

He glanced around. The bar was almost empty. 'Sure it is.' He came out from behind the counter and held me in a strong, firm grip. The muscled grip of a grown son.

I heard myself say: 'It must have been his heart.'

But that's how everyone dies, isn't it? Their heart stops.

I began to cry, then I tore myself away.

In the departure lounge people were laughing, chatting, scrolling through their emails, re-packing their carry-on baggage, stirring their coffee, texting. Maybe they were excited about the journey: the kind of journey you might return from and say, 'It was the holiday of a lifetime.' Or anxious: they had to give a professional presentation and they were ill-prepared, or they were going to meet an estranged sister for the first time in years. They were getting on with their lives, in a normal world.

In his poem 'The Musee des Beaux Arts', W.H. Auden describes how the painter Breughel depicts Icarus' spectacular fall as invisible or irrelevant to those around him:

. . . the ploughman may
Have heard the splash, the forsaken cry,
But for him it was not an important failure; the sun shone
As it had to on the white legs disappearing into the green
Water, and the expensive delicate ship that must have seen
Something amazing, a boy falling out of the sky,
Had somewhere to get to and sailed calmly on.

My fellow-passengers had places to go too. They didn't know what I was going through, and even if they did, what would they do? Young men die every day and if you don't know them, you don't imagine their forsaken cry as they fall from the sky into the green water. Why would you? Like the ship, you sail calmly on.

On the plane I had three seats to myself. I'd told the airline staff what had happened and that I needed space, but the flight was half empty. I was glad I could cry alone, without needing to explain. The word 'bereft' came to me. The stewardess assigned to my section of the plane was a good fairy: gentle, beautiful, considerate, sisterly. She asked what she could do to help me. What I wanted most was Raph, alive. I wanted not to be bereft.

Bring my son back, I thought. Not possible.

'A glass of red wine,' I told her. I wanted to finish what I'd started at the bar.

But I couldn't. This was Emirates, and she was sorry, but they didn't serve alcohol. 'You just relax, Madam. We'll get you there safely.'

'I don't want to get there safely,' I didn't say. 'I want this plane to crash. I want the engines to fail right now. Fuck the other passengers. I'm done.'

Instead, I reached for another kind of comfort: the comfort that had saved me before, and that will save me for as long as my mind is still mine. Words metabolise thought, and as I lay across three seats in the dark and opened the notebook on my phone, they came instinctively. I didn't know why some of them were addressed to Raph, and some were addressed to those he'd left behind. But afterwards, when language failed me completely, I'd be glad to have had such an overriding impulse to express what was, and remains, inexpressible. Later still, I would come to think that he joined me during those endless hours of limbo and wrote his own farewell.

In Dubai, during a four-hour stopover, there was still no booze, so I drank a green smoothie in a space-age bar with an air-con chill so cold I shivered. Was it hot outside, at whatever time of day or night this was? What season was it in Dubai? The smoothie tasted of seaweed and dung. It struck me that I'd chosen it not because it looked appetising but because it was what Raphaël would have chosen. On the wall-screen a promo for Dubai, with a fake Greta Thunberg voice-over, was running on a loop. They'd used a sound-alike to flog the 'dreams' and the 'wonder' of a territory with one of the biggest per capita CO_2 emissions in the world.

Dear friends, I wrote. *This is the hardest news any parent can receive, and the hardest to pass on.* I sent it in batches through a blizzard of tears, attaching the words I wrote to Raph. Or from Raph. Or with Raph. I still don't know which.

Shock is the body's way of protecting you from pain. It's why you can make calls to your family breaking the news and book a flight on which you write a letter to your dead son and then throw a series of hand grenades through the ether telling friends and family that a baby whose nappy they changed is dead. A boy they climbed trees with is dead. A child actor they worked with is dead. A teenager they skateboarded and did gymnastics with is dead. A zoology student they studied vipers with and danced all night with is dead. A conservationist they tracked a jaguar with is dead. An activist they were arrested with and who cheered them up in the police van is dead. A partner they loved with all their heart and saw a future with is dead.

Nothing much came out of me for a long time after I sent that mass mail. I stumbled about like a sleepwalker, and when I bumped into the thing that called itself reality I recoiled in horror. My voice wasn't mine, and my mouth tasted of ashes. I had nothing to say to the wider world and couldn't imagine a time when I would. Communication itself felt overrated, and even if I'd had the urge to share something, I couldn't have strung together a single thought, let alone a sentence. I had always relied on language to access my thoughts. But words had simply stopped working.

I fell apart.

CHAPTER 2: WILL YOU MAKE PLANS?

How do we become who we are today, and then the next version of ourselves, and the next, and the next? How much is down to the accretion of experience, how much to chance, how much to the road consciously taken or the road consciously resisted, and how much purely and simply to a sense of purpose? 'Tell me,' wrote the poet Mary Oliver, 'what is it you plan to do / with your one wild and precious life?' It's a question I asked myself frequently, and with increasing intensity, in the weeks and months that followed.

My father worked as a craftsman, and when Raphaël was three, he made him a wooden ark. It was a floating animal sanctuary, a larder, a breeding-ground, a time-capsule, a social science experiment, a panic room – and a toybox. It was unseaworthy, but Raphaël didn't care. He loved filling it with mammals, insects, sea creatures and birds, which he'd name as he marched them up the gang-plank. Dinosaurs went in there too. He didn't know about the aeons of deep time that preceded and followed them, let alone extinction. Everything he loved was now, and alive, and drew breath. And he knew instinctively – as perhaps all children do – that he, too, was an animal. Growing up, many of us disconnect from our innate creaturehood. I know I did. But Raphaël never lost sight of his.

There were many steps along his path to activism: demonstrating against tuition fees in Britain as a teenager; digesting the mind-bending scale of mass extinction during his four years as a zoology student; working as a wildlife biologist and journalist in endangered habitats across the world. But it began on a small scale. He'd watch woodlice, squirrels and foxes in the garden, and study our three cats. For his fifth birthday we bought him a fish tank. Later there were gerbils and, later still, horned lizards.

In a quirk of fate, his first adult immersion in what he came to call the Wild was on a wildlife programme in Limpopo: the district where, seven years later, he would die. In the intervening time he studied zoology and worked or volunteered on wildlife conservation projects and at animal rescue centres in Latin and South America, the US and Southeast Asia. And the more evidence of cruelty and injustice and ecocide he witnessed, the more his commitment grew to rescue what he could.

It was in Central and South America and in Southeast Asia that he first became aware of the extent of illegal wildlife trading. There was no avoiding it. In market after market, he saw the body parts of bears, armadillos and pangolins openly on sale alongside caged big cats, monkeys, rare birds, bears and snakes – many of which would end up abandoned and unable to survive in the wild. It enraged him, and he resolved to do all he could to fight what has become a multi-billion-dollar industry.

Mark Twain said that the two most important days of your life are the day you are born and the day you know why. By the time he went to university, Raphaël had a sense of purpose. 'I believe that when you feel you belong in a place,' he wrote, 'it's because you need to be there. Things depend on you being there and doing whatever it is you're supposed to do. But if you leave the place you belong, the world doesn't quite keep spinning the way it used to. The longer you're not where you belong doing what you're supposed to do, the worse it gets. That's how you know where you need to be.'

In his four years as a student zoologist he made deep friendships that would last the rest of his life, founded the international wildlife workers' group the Wildwork, organised happenings, took up with a beautiful girl, worked in bars, practised parkour and gymnastics, turned himself into an astonishing dancer – and drank. Oh, how he drank. They all did. There's a video of him doing the 'Neck Challenge', which I watch when I need him to make me laugh. He mixes fruit, shampoo, booze and spices into a smoothie, chugs it all down in one go, then goes outside to perform a series of high-risk flips and somersaults on the dark winter lawn.

He spent most of his third year doing fieldwork at a conservation project in Central America. Costa Rica is one of the world's few environmental success stories. Not only does almost all its energy come from renewable sources, but it's also the only tropical country that has managed to reverse deforestation: trees now cover more than half its land. But despite this, it was here that Raphaël saw at first hand the role of human activity in the devastating annihilation of animal and plant species that is the Sixth Mass Extinction.

In Tortuguero National Park he studied jaguar tracks, measured the wingspans of bats and took extensive notes for his dissertation on the exquisite camouflage techniques of the eyelash palm pit-viper. On the beaches he counted turtles and their eggs: when the mothers had finished laying, his team would measure them with massive aluminium callipers, check them for injuries, attach tags to their flippers and leave coded, poacher-proof signs about the nest's location. One of his best photos, which accompanied his first ever article in a zoological magazine, is emblematic of the complexities of all Earth's ecosystems. It shows a tiny turtle hatchling resting in a depression in the sand made by the imprint of a jaguar's paw: a neat illustration of how one endangered species kills and eats another. But jaguars were not the worst predators. On the beaches and in the local markets, the poaching industry thrived. Raphaël and his team would spend their evenings preserving turtle nests − while a few miles away traders were openly selling stolen eggs, destined never to hatch. He understood the need of local people in areas of threatened biodiversity to make a living, but he raged at the way the placebo effect, coupled with centuries of cultural belief, was massacring some of the planet's most threatened species. He knew that as long as people believe that concoctions made of powdered rhino horn, pangolin parts, armadillo scales, and the bile of bears and tigers are actually effective, there will be a market for them. And until those beliefs are relegated to the past they will exact a brutal cost. It tortured him.

While he wrestled with the problem of animal trafficking, he championed sanctuaries where the animals were happy and well-cared for enough to breed. One such place was a tiger sanctuary at a Buddhist temple in Thailand, whose big cat population had grown by word of mouth after the first abandoned tiger cub was handed to the care of the monks. Vets' fees and meat were expensive, and tourism ensured a steady income for the temple. Volunteers like Raphaël would meditate with the monks every morning before going about their duties, which included cleaning shit from the enclosures, playing with adult tigers and bottle-feeding cubs.

But in 2016 the temple hit the news in a way that shook his faith in humankind. Months after his last visit, Raphaël learned that the temple had been raided by the Thai authorities, who claimed it was trading in animal parts. Raphaël couldn't believe it and was distraught. Worse, they seized all the 147 tigers, and transported them to a government facility with much smaller enclosures and no enrichment.

'They're going to die in that place,' he said.

And he was right. Within three years, more than half of them had perished.

Bewildered and angry, he spent months ruminating over what had gone so grotesquely wrong at the temple – and reluctantly concluded that someone with access to it had committed crimes. But he was also furious about the online campaign against the temple that precipitated the raid, because its organisers must have known that in government custody, the tigers' lives would be endangered.

And that previously contented, healthy animals that Raphaël and other volunteers had loved and cared for would be doomed to suffer and die in terrible conditions.

For a long time he raged and grieved. But slowly, his despair turned to resolution, and he began filming interviews for an investigative documentary on Southeast Asian animal sanctuaries and their link to the illegal wildlife trade. And he threw himself into what he always said was the best antidote to depression that exists: activism.

When Extinction Rebellion exploded into existence in 2018, he'd found his tribe. Within weeks of attending his first meeting, he was running XR's fledgling social media team, where he wrote blogs, live-streamed from major events, took part in protests and masterminded the Paint the Streets campaign, which runs to this day. I'll never know how many times he was arrested, but his commitment to such an evidently vital cause made me feel that I'd stood on the sidelines for too long. It was time to become involved in something big and meaningful. The realisation came at a time when I was feeling deeply unsettled by Amitav Ghosh's book *The Great Derangement*, which criticised literature's failure to reflect and address the breakdown of Earth systems on anything approaching the scale required. Ghosh was right – but I wanted him to be wrong. So in the summer of 2019, I joined an online exchange with a couple of other writers who shared my concerns. Our initial conversations revolved around how to engage our creative writing students and fellow writers in environmentalism. But our good intentions felt tame – until I called Raph. Quickly, the energy changed. As Writers Rebel, we began planning a pop-up literary event as part of XR's upcoming October Rebellion, and soon forty of Britain's leading literary figures had volunteered to perform to the public from a soapbox on an illegally held site. When Margaret Atwood sent her blessings we felt another shift.

On the morning of our gig, I escaped the the crush of protesters in Trafalgar Square to meet Raphaël in a café on Charing Cross Road. He was evading the police and had the phone number of the XR legal team inked on his arm in case he was arrested. He sat on his phone and, switching to French, he told me some of what he'd been up to – including running the team that had sealed off and occupied the square where we and others would be performing. He drew me a map on a napkin to show how they'd pulled it off, and as he spoke I was struck by the way our relationship was quietly entering a new dimension. We were no longer just mother and son, but two people committed to a cause that both eclipsed and filled us. I sensed a new kind of future for us both: a future that contained hardship, joy, disappointment, euphoria, anxiety, pride, fellowship, purpose and a thousand other things that we had yet to encounter. And when we hugged goodbye, I felt ready for all of it.

Raw, urgent, scrappy and completely electric, the gig was nothing like any literary festival any of us had been involved in before. A 300-strong audience packed the pavement, and functioned as a human roadblock as the sun shone and the police looked on, some with interest, others with bored bemusement. When it started to pour with rain, we decamped to the shelter of a nearby archway and carried on. It felt like a small moment in British literary history, and it made us hopeful that more writers would come to apply the 'existential creativity' Ben Okri calls for when he asks: 'If you knew you were at the last days of the human story, what would you write?'

Within months, we had a social media following, a website and a newsletter, and we were publishing weekly blogs. In January 2020, as I gathered a small team to work on what would become the Rebel Library, Raphaël and I spoke on WhatsApp and exchanged emails and documents more often than we'd ever done before – he in London and I in Los Angeles. He was running ten kilometres a day in preparation for his South African trip. He was drafting a Crowdfunder campaign for his anti-poaching film. He was building up the Wildwork, which had 12,000 members and was rapidly expanding. He had two court cases on the horizon: one for obstructing Trafalgar Square, another for vandalising the Brazilian Embassy in London in protest at Brazil's trashing of the Amazon rainforest. And he was deep into writing what was to be his last article, campaigning for voting rights for children from the age of sixteen.

'One of the most viscerally, fundamentally unjust rules in our societies is that future generations have no say,' he wrote. 'Young people whose future is being destroyed have no political power - not even the right to vote for change. But what could happen if future generations had a say in the world they'll inherit? What if we did something moving, challenging and daring? What if – all around the world – young people queued together at the polling stations, demanding their right to participate in democracy?'

Just before he left, he sent me his latest draft to edit. How full of plans we were. And how aligned those plans seemed to be. It felt that something new was unfolding, rapidly. It made me excited for the future.

CHAPTER 3: WILL YOU FACE WHAT YOU MUST?

In Johannesburg, officials boarded the plane and pointed laser thermometers at our foreheads. I heard the word 'Covid'. Surely it had barely left China yet? My son was dead, and they were worrying about a *virus*?

As I stepped on solid ground and entered the airport his death felt so real it choked me. I was spinning out.

A few days ago, he'd arrived at this airport with his hand luggage too. Queued for the same immigration process. Probably checked his phone like I was doing.

And only yesterday he'd been alive.

He'd been planning the trip for a month and I knew he was excited. But the days leading up to his departure had been busy, frantic and anxious: as usual, he had too much to do and not enough time to do it in, and when he'd finally launched the Crowdfunder he was deluged with messages to say the donation system had a glitch.

I checked his last WhatsApp message. His course had begun and I'd asked how it was going.

'Yeah enjoying it. Bit apprehensive.'

When I saw that his message was dated February 5th, a jolt went through me. He'd felt apprehensive the day before he died. Why didn't he listen to that apprehension, and why didn't I pay it more attention, instead of just writing words that now made me cringe: 'I get that you're feeling apprehensive. Keep a cool head and don't rush into anything just for the sake of having an experience.'

'What is the purpose of your visit, madam?' asked the immigration officer, not looking up.

I hadn't expected this. I stalled. It felt too shocking to say aloud. Finally I said, 'I've come to fetch my son's body.'

His hand hovered over the form he was filling out. Still not looking up, he scribbled something very fast, said, 'Keep this with your passport,' and gestured me through. Later, when I glanced at what he'd written under Purpose of Visit, I felt for him. It *was* too shocking.

He'd simply written 'VISIT'.

★

It had been raining, and harsh sunlight glinted on the puddles. After twenty-seven hours of travelling across multiple timezones, the disorienting shift of hour and temperature were part of a nightmarish season all its own, with no clear characteristics, no rules, no logic and no end.

On the hotel shuttle I checked my feed. Extinction Rebellion was grieving. Among the messages of despair and shock and love was a link to a fresh news story. On the 6th of February, the night Raph died, an urban fox slipped into Portcullis House in Parliament, made its way up four flights of stairs and shat copiously on the floor. Someone has sent me a clip of the animal being released by security guards. As it emerges from the carboard box, it looks disoriented for a moment. Then it gets its bearings and trots off into the London night.

When it came to slipping into Parliament and causing a stir, Raphaël had experience. In April 2019, XR staged one of its most attention-grabbing actions. In what became known as the Naked Protest, rebels posing as visitors to the public gallery interrupted a Brexit debate by stripping off to reveal naked bodies covered in slogans and symbols of elephants, signifying the elephant in the room: the rolling ecological and atmospheric crisis. Having glued their hands to the glass of the public gallery, they spent thirty minutes with their buttocks and breasts bared to the chamber. Iggy Fox was there, secretly filming while posing as a tourist. The footage he smuggled out went viral and brought a smile to many faces.

So an urban fox entering a parliament and shitting on the floor just hours after he died was seized on by many of his fellow activists as classic Iggy: an audacious dirty protest from beyond the grave.

But Iggy Fox didn't do woo-woo. And nor did Raph. And I didn't either. If science can't prove something, it's just a theory.

What a neat story, I thought, bleakly. *What a cute coincidence.*

Later, my thoughts on coincidence, and the possibility that consciousness continues after the body dies, would become bolder.

Not a coincidence, a voice called Raphaël would start whispering. *I was there. I did it.*

The last time I'd seen Michel was at Matti's graduation in Edinburgh, and the last time we'd communicated was in October the previous year, when we'd exchanged anxious emails after I'd chanced on a BBC news clip showing Raphaël being arrested after gluing himself to a scaffold in Trafalgar Square. But now, in the hotel lobby, instinctively, Michel, Matti and I had time-travelled back two decades and were hugging tightly in a threesome. This was once our family hug, when there were four of us.

Our eyes raw from sleeplessness and crying, we went for a meal, flipping between French and English the way we always had. There was an understanding that we had a mission, and we'd complete it. Outside it looked like noon but it felt more like evening or dawn. And somewhere, of course, it was. All over the world, people were opening their inboxes and getting the news. They were crying. They were numb with shock. They were saying it couldn't be true. They were remembering their last conversation with him. They were writing him an email that he'd never open. They were trying to phone him because they couldn't believe it. But he wasn't picking up.

I'd thrown a bomb.

'There are no words to express . . .' was a frequent line in the messages that began to pour in. It was true. There were no words to express. But people tried, and I was grateful that they did. One writer, admired for his sophisticated prose, wrote simply: 'Fuck, fuck, fuck!'

Another sent me what the grieving Wordsworth wrote after the death of his six-year-old son: 'I loved the Boy with the utmost love of which my soul is capable, and he is taken from me – yet in the agony of my spirit in surrendering such a treasure I feel a thousand times richer than if I had never possessed it.'

Another sent a quotation from Mary Oliver's 'The Uses of Sorrow':

Someone I loved once gave me a box full of darkness.
It took me years to understand that this, too, was a gift.

I wondered about this box of darkness. How many years would I have to wait before it felt like a gift?

Another sent me the Bantu word *ubuntu*. It means 'I am because you are; you are because I am.' And now he was not, what was I, and what was he? And where were any of us? I didn't know. Grief had kicked me to the floor and was still kicking. My ribcage felt bruised; my organs naked, pulsing and unprotected. I wanted to be anyone but me. *Make it stop, Raph*, I begged. But he couldn't. And what kind of monster would I be if I didn't feel this level of pain? It kept on kicking.

The next morning, we took the only flight to the town of Hoedspruit, where one of the directors of the anti-poaching course would be waiting for us. There was no difficulty spotting him. A young white man, heavily muscled, he was an emergency flare of anxiety and distress.

'Nothing like this has ever happened before,' he said as he shouldered my bag, fighting back tears.

'It's not your fault,' I told him. 'We know that.'

He buckled with relief. Saying it had cost me nothing

and I could see it had lifted a colossal weight. We could go to the morgue to see his body as soon as there was a visiting pathologist available, he told us – though when this might be wasn't clear. And tomorrow, if his baby hadn't been born – it was due any day – he'd be the one to take us to the savannah where Raphaël died to meet the course instructors who were with him and the chief paramedic who came to the scene. A baby, I thought. Raphaël would like that. Someone new coming along, so soon after he's left.

We installed ourselves in a villa on the nature reserve like a family on a safari trip. We'd been shaken before – by crises, betrayals, divorce and other deaths – but not like this. The next morning the course director drove us through flat savannah, flat-topped trees, red earth and quietness. The air felt surreally warm after the cold of Texas. However long we stayed here, I realised, I would never get my bearings.

We greeted the two instructors who had been with Raphaël when he collapsed, and they offered shaky condolences. They told us their names, which I forgot immediately. Later I asked them again, and wrote them down, and then lost the piece of paper. The men spoke alternately, as if they were a single unit cleaved in two by pain.

'He was on the ground. He was having trouble breathing. He was disoriented. But it was like he was still singing,' said one. 'Like he was still trying to sing. He was confused. He was crawling along, making these noises.'

I seized on this. Of course he was still trying to sing. In his head he was still running, still happy, still singing. *He didn't know he was dying.* This thought was important to me. *He didn't know.* But I knew that at some point he would have been in pain. I could think about that pain: about how violently he suffered, and for how long. But in a flash of clear-headedness, and with the conviction that Raphaël would want it, I made a choice. I would never think about it. Ever. His pain was simply off the table. It was the least important thing about his death, just as the pain of being born was the least important thing about his life.

The paramedics were there within ten minutes, the men told us.

'They lifted him onto the bed of the truck, by that marula tree.' One of them pointed to a tree set apart from the others, like a landmark, and we walked over to it. The Death Tree, I thought. It wasn't striking, like a flame tree or a baobab. It had the generic look of a tree a child might draw. I fingered a clutch of its leathery leaves and pulled some off. Another jeep pulled up, and the chief paramedic introduced himself. He looked and sounded aghast, as though it had only just happened.

'I was sure we were going to save him,' he said. 'But it happened very fast. It took twenty minutes from the time he collapsed to the time we lost him.'

Michel is an epidemiologist, but he trained as a doctor. Soon he and the paramedic were deep in a medical conversation about the possible causes: was it snakebite, a double pneumothorax, a deep vein thrombosis, a heart anomaly? It wasn't that I didn't want to know why our healthy son, who had never been fitter in his life, collapsed and perished from one moment to the next. But part of me thought dully: *It doesn't matter. It's too late. He's dead. The question isn't how Raphaël died, but how we go on living.* I had other questions though. Did Raphaël know he was dead? Where was he now, and how was he doing?

In the short time we'd been here the temperature had risen to thirty-six degrees and just then, for a brief moment, I felt a shimmer that seemed to be Raph, or his essence. *He's here,* I thought. *Right next to us.* A magical thought, of course. Matti was moving further and further away from the conversation about blood pressure, pupils like pinpricks, lungs failing, pulse dropping, heart giving out, pupils fully dilated, repeated defibrillation. I joined him. We were both grateful, as we half-listened, to have so little medical knowledge. In that moment, we'd have preferred to have had none.

'I don't just feel like an only child. I feel like a lonely child,' said Matti, and my heart broke all over again. Our pain was not the same. In the reconfiguration of his family map, we were all new people. We were all lost and diminished, but Matti was lost and diminished in the way only a bereaved sibling can be when they're suddenly the last one standing. With the brother with whom he could share twenty-five years of memories and parent jokes gone from the equation, Matti's square had become a triangle.

'Remember how you always used to ask me, "If me and Raphaël are standing on the edge of a cliff, which one would you push off, if you had to?" And I always gave you the same answer?' He nodded. I'd always said, 'Neither. I'd jump myself.' Because the death of either would be an annihilation. 'It was true then, and it's true now,' I told him.

'I know, Ma,' said Matti wearily. I was glad he knew it, but it didn't help him. In that moment, nothing could. I stroked the rough, warm trunk of the Death Tree. I saw now that it was in fact two trees, a marula and an umbrella thorn intertwined, their trunks and branches almost indistinguishable. I knew there must be a metaphor there – an obvious one – but I didn't have the energy to find it. Later I would learn that the marula tree is common in the savannah. That it's typically found growing alongside umbrella thorns, also known as acacias. That its leaves can relieve heartburn. That its bark contains antihistamines, and that if you crush it and mix it with water you can use it to treat dysentery and diarrhoea, and as a malaria prophylactic. So the Death Tree was a medicine tree.

Some hours later, we travelled by jeep through the fever dream of the savannah past trees blazing with orange flowers, past skeins of squawking birds rising through the shimmer of the heat, to a wooden hangar where the other participants on the course were waiting to meet us. They'd all been with him when he fell.

'They're all in shock. So you'll find them a bit quiet,' the course director warned us at the door. 'But they all think Raphaël would have seen the course through to the end. He quickly established himself as the leader. He was a pretty committed and determined guy.' Michel and I glanced at each other. If he hadn't been a committed and determined guy, he'd never have become an activist, never have wanted to make that documentary, never have come here. And he'd still be alive. Or we'd have had him longer. 'They've decided they're going to carry his kit bag with them wherever they go. They'll take turns to carry it. They want him to finish the course.'

We told him that Raphaël would want that too.

Inside the hangar, it was dark. As my eyes adjusted I made out rows of young people at rough wooden desks, and a projector. They were just back from a run: they were sweaty, and filthy with mud and dust and blood. Like Raphaël, they had all recently shaved their heads. The twenty-five guys and one girl, Black and white in equal numbers, looked drained and miserable and some were clearly on the verge

33

of tears. They were tenderly young, and every one of them was beautiful. Tragedy had given their faces a cast you seldom see in the young. I wondered how many of them had come this close to sudden death before.

Mustering an impromptu double-act, Michel and I told them how proud we were of Raphaël, who came here because he was determined to devote his energy to what mattered most to him. When we spoke about his commitment to protecting wildlife species and habitats through conservation work and activism, they nodded in recognition. They knew. Of course they knew. As we spoke, our voices shook a little, but we didn't break down, and when we screened the short film Raph had made about the Wildwork a lightness entered the room and our faces lifted, because somehow he was here again, belonging in his own skin, and belonging with us. When it was over, they smiled and cheered, and I went round the room and hugged them one by one. In every hug I could feel their longing for their own families. Most of them apologised for being covered in sweat or blood but I didn't care. I was hugging them for me, and for them, but most of all I was giving them each the hug that Raph would give them, if he could. And in every embrace, he felt alive. Somehow, in those fifteen minutes, Raphaël had been with us again.

★

Exhausted from the day, Matti and I stand on the veranda at the villa while Michel makes calls. And suddenly I've had enough. This is a joke, and Raph's taken it too far.

'Raph, stop messing around! We've had enough of this shit! Come back!' I call into the trees.

'He's gone, Ma,' says Matti, taking a drag of his cigarette.

'Do you really believe that?'

'No. But I will when I see his body.'

I feel the same way. I'm yearning to see him because it means I'll be with him again – even though he's now a corpse. *Corpse*. The word alone makes me feel physically sick.

'Just come back, Raph!' I yell again.

Suddenly there is a flash of russet in the branches opposite: a small bird with a theatrically long tail. Instead of flying from one place to another, it flutters around in a little circle for a few seconds as if saying *look at me* – then disappears into the foliage. I catch my breath. And then I laugh. I'd never seen a bird behave like that before. And how many birds with sweeping tails exactly the colour of Raph's long russet braid have we seen since we arrived? And how many creatures have we seen putting on a performance? None.

I turn to Matti. 'Don't tell me that's not a sign!'

'OK, Ma, I won't tell you it's not a sign,' he says, blowing out smoke.

But I know it means something. I can't explain the feeling rationally, because intuition isn't rational. I read once that after a mother gives birth, some of the baby's foetal cells remain in her blood for the rest of her life. If that's so, my Raph-cells are stirring. Violently.

'Come on, Matti. A creature with a long red tail, showing off? How could it not be Raph?' *How could it not be Icarus, the man who became a bird?*

Matti shakes his head. He is a creative rationalist. Trained as a mechanical engineer, he designs nuclear fusion reactors for a living. Science has neither been able to validate or disprove that other dimensions co-exist with the world we know. But if it is ever proven, until there is also proof that the membranes that separate us can be breached, he doesn't believe in signs.

Nor did I, until a minute ago. The shift is marked by a subtle physical sensation, like a sudden change in temperature or pressure, or the pull of an urgent question. I have two options. I could ignore this feeling, and continue to put all my faith in mechanistic logic. Or I could explore it, and become open to the idea that there is more to existence than what science can identify and measure.

Raphaël was very good at being alive. So why shouldn't he also be very good at being dead?

If grief has blown my mind open, I don't intend to close it.

CHAPTER 4: WILL YOU FILL UP YOUR LIFE?

When I was pregnant with Raphaël, I knew that climatologists feared the twenty-first century would bring runaway global heating. But I didn't agonise about the world that he and his brother would grow up in. The next century, though close, still felt theoretical, and my mind was on other things. I was writing a comic novel about evolution and humankind's relationship to the nonhuman world, and exploring how full of fantasy, delusion and grandiosity our species is, how ruled by our lizard brains, our patriarchal gods and our life-sucking economic paradigms – and yet how capable of compassion, of tenderness, of love, of art, of moral vision. Back then, ecological devastation and climate tipping-points didn't feature on the news, which was dominated by more immediate and graspable dramas: the bloodbath in the Balkans, the massacre in Rwanda, Mandela's election as South African president, the historic ceasefire in Northern Ireland and Russia's attack on Chechnya.

My contractions begin on the 29th of September, which is St Raphaël's day, although I don't know it, and soon after midnight on September 30th, there he is, purplish-white, emitting deep, otherworldly cries. He looks both brand new and ancient, innocent and wise, trailing vernix and blood as though freshly disembarked from some primal, organic chariot. Like his brother, like all of us, he has overcome the incalculable odds of his cells never having existed at all. My friend Polly's son Gabriel was born three weeks earlier. Without discussing it, we've named them both after archangels. Later Raphaël chooses his own winged name: Icarus.

Later still he shortens it to Iggy, and when he becomes an activist he takes on the surname Fox, because he's grown up with a troupe of fellow-redheads: me, his brother, and the scrappy, ingenious urban foxes that visit the garden almost daily. The name suits him. He spends hours designing the Icarus wing tattoo which begins on his shoulder blade as a piece of engineering and morphs into the scythe of a bird wing on his bicep. From the impossible piece of bird anatomy, a single feather has come loose and is falling.

His first word is 'Matti'. His second word is 'yes'. Mummy and Papa come later. Then 'no', in French. Firmly. *Non*. He's an oral baby. Food in, words out. Early on he learns the animal noises: the cow's moo, the cat's meow, the dog's bark, the fish's mouth going *pop pop pop*. We love the way his fat little lips form the silent, plosive sound. *Do the fish!* we urge him. *Do the fish!* He flexes his tiny starfish hand and clenches it around strawberries, melon chunks, bananas, croissants, and watches them squish.

He crawls on all fours without using his knees, nappied bum high in the air.

At ten and a half months, at our family home in France, he is playing on the floor with a plastic stegosaurus. He burps, laughs and carries on playing. Then, moments later, as if he has finally processed it, he utters his first sentence. In three words, he reveals he's not just observant of the body's workings but a tiny person who is aware of time.

In his unnaturally deep baby-voice, he informs the stegosaurus:

'Sometimes I burp.'

Two summers later, he meets death for the first time.

He comes indoors with a great tit cupped gently in his tiny, grubby hands. 'I found a sleeping bird,' he says.

When we tell him it will never wake again, he's shocked
– and inconsolable. We hold a funeral and a burial. Not
a bird any more, we tell him. Underground, it will rot
and magic into something else. But this makes no sense
to him. He puts snail shells on the little grave and howls.

He is naturally curious, but he seldom asks questions,
as his brother does incessantly: instead, he considers something and offers his theory. The moon switches on and
off like a light bulb. If I keep digging this hole, I'll get to
Australia. Squirrels act crazy because they're drunk on
rotten apple juice.

From the age of two, the only thing, apart from Matti,
that will bring him down from his spectacular, seizure-like
tantrums is what we call Raph's Squid Video: a David
Attenborough documentary about cephalopods. When he
watches it, he looks like a fiery-haired gnome, rigid with
concentrated awe as an animated Architeuthis attacks a
whale five times its size, latching on with its suckers, then
pulsing its titanic body and streaming through the darkness.
It should be terrifying for a child his age, but he's more
mesmerised than scared. Those deep-sea creatures seem to
tell him something that no human can.

From babyhood, Raphaël navigates his world through
Matti, who is his third parent and his mind-reader: a mini
psychologist who can always intuit what he wants, loves
or fears. Later, as teenagers, their differences will matter

increasingly to them both. But as a young child, Matti is the family member Raphaël connects with most instinctively: the one he most ardently admires and most loyally emulates. And Raphaël is Matti's beloved, adorable and often wildly irritating little friend.

He knows himself young. He insists on dressing himself from the age of three. From early on, he knows that clothes signal identity, and he has firm opinions about his. He'll choose three T-shirts and wear them one on top of the other. There's a photo of him with a huge white owl perched on his arm, taken on the day the raptor man visits the school. His T-shirt is both back to front and inside-out, with the label showing. I want to tell his primary teachers: it's not neglect, it's pig-headedness! As an adolescent and adult, he stocks his wardrobe from charity shops. He loves torn jeans, vests, waistcoats, fake fur and look-at-me hats, and is defiantly attached to a green fake leather jacket which everyone who loves him begs him not to wear. LIVE FAST, DIE YOUNG, says one of his T-shirts.

Be nice, I say to Matti ten times a day.

To Raphaël I say, just as often: *be normal*.

To his credit, he never listens. He just laughs.

He is the more hedonistic of the brothers. He loves to smell and taste unlikely things, and mix substances to see what happens. At the age of seven he makes popcorn on the gas ring, refusing all help. As a teenager he bakes cakes and flapjacks, concocts spiced fruit jams, dries mint for tea, snorts nutmeg – and once, disastrously, chilli powder. He can put a lit match in his mouth and close it. He can blow smoke rings. Later, he adds micro-dosing on psylocibin and LSD to his repertoire.

'You know Ma,' Matti tells me one day, 'Raph actually likes shitting. And he always tells everyone when he's got a boner. Then one time we smelled something bad and Raph said it smells just like the cheese in your belly button. Gross! Who smells the cheese in their belly button?'

Raph, is who.

Any divorce is wrenching, and ours is no exception. By the end of the century, with two school-age boys, Michel and I have weathered some rocky years and entered the state of exhausted stagnation we see in other couples around us. Like them, we schlep to counselling. But in our case, the dismal hours spent in a pastel-wallpapered room with a kind lady and a box of tissues for the emotionally overwhelmed fail to help.

When we tell the boys we are divorcing Matti becomes anxious, miserable and angry. I argue that our marriage will only get worse if we stay together, like my parents did. But even if he senses this is true, we have still upended his world. Raphaël, too young to fully understand, takes the news with more equanimity at first. 'My parents have split up,' I hear him tell a classmate – almost as a boast. His best friend Saskia's parents have just separated too, so it seems he is framing divorce as something parents just do, that their kids must just get used to. Our family, like Saskia's, has simply undergone a category shift. But soon enough it sinks in.

I try to make our new, much smaller home appealing to the boys in the alternate weeks when they are with me. There is a green space across the street, and a park up the road with a river running through it: here they fish for minnows and stickleback to stock the pond we create in the back garden, where they spend hours playing. But there is no way round them having to share a room, which they both resent, and they are fractious and increasingly at one another's throats.

Then, the month after we move in, my father has a bad fall. He goes to hospital, but he doesn't improve and the doctors think he might have cancer. He is in excruciating pain and can't walk. It gets worse. After a tortuous three weeks, he sinks into a coma and dies of what later emerges to be septicaemia contracted in the hospital. On top of my guilt over the divorce, I am now in deep grief. The boys, who loved their funny, irascible Danish grandfather, share it. That summer, they have endured their parents' split, their first bereavement and a move to a part-time home. It happens in the space of three months and they have no say in any of it. I feel like the world's worst mother. On a hunch that it will boost their confidence, I sign them up for weekly judo lessons, and soon they're in little white suits, enthusiastically flinging other kids around on mats and competing in matches. But they're deeply scarred, and that summer takes a heavy toll on both of them. On top of everything else, Raphaël is moving to the same secondary school as his brother. He's been happy at his primary school, a short walk from home, and although he'll keep up his local friendships this represents yet another change of world – and culture.

But slowly, the boys emerge from their misery. Raphaël settles in at the new school, and Carsten, who I have met at a literary festival in Canada, slowly becomes a fixture in the family equation. On our visits to Denmark, Raphaël and Carsten's six-year-old daughter Laura are soon communicating in a hybrid language that Raphaël calls 'blibber-blobber', and Matti, a natural linguist, picks up Danish fast. The day he escorts Laura round a funfair trail on a little pony, then announces to her in perfect Danish, as it pees: *'Din hest har en stor tissemand'* ('Your horse has a big willy') I know that even though we can't all live together, we have become a step-family.

Both boys are natural performers, but at the age of eight Raphaël's life takes a wild and unexpected swerve when he is spotted by a casting director looking for child actors for the movie *Nanny McPhee*. He attends the twelve auditions with a fierce determination to land a part – which makes sense, after all he's been through. Here is something that can give him agency beyond his reconfigured family and his huge, alarming school: something that can be his alone.

Due to his preternaturally adult seriousness he is cast as Eric, the 'little professor', and by the spring of 2004 he's become one of the seven Brown children, and is being measured for a russet three-piece suit and other miniature costumes. The kids quickly learn the rules: enjoy the work, but take it seriously; never look at the camera; and above all, don't 'act'. It's a four-month shoot, with schooling on set and a sugar ban, and although they often laugh until they cry, there are flashpoints of stress and many hours of boredom. And mortifyingly, Raphaël is tempestuous from the start. He is a natural in front of the camera, and takes direction well, but within two weeks he comes close to being sacked for getting into a fight with one of the other kids. And on the day that word comes over the walkie-talkies that a child has been electrocuted, nobody needs to ask which one. It isn't serious. He just wanted to know if the warnings about the cattle-fence were justified.

When it's over and the movie is showing in cinemas, he's upset about the envious taunts in the school playground, and ambivalent about the praise, but he is proud to have worked professionally, and to have made money that he can use when he is older. He's always been a tiny kid, dwarfed by his contemporaries, and relying on his humour and charisma to claim his space. But after *Nanny McPhee*, he talks and behaves like a taller, older boy.

'I definitely don't want to be an actor when I'm grown-up,' he announces. I breathe an inward sigh of relief that the experiment is over. 'But I want to do it again, while I'm still a child.'

My heart sinks a little, but he's firm about it.

He goes to more auditions, and his next features are American horror movies shot in Bulgaria. Thanks to Cartoon Network, the accent doesn't faze him. He plays the orphaned kid who yells 'Watch out!'; the bereaved kid who blames his mother for his father's gory death; the kid in the wheelchair who is pushed down the stairs by a terrifying humanoid; the resilient survivor kid who emerges from a burning house against the odds. The budgets are small, and the sets far less lavish than on *Nanny McPhee*: an old paper mill full of ancient props, with rats and feral dogs scavenging for scraps by the catering vans; a mock-up of an Arizona home, with cacti and dried peppers hanging on the walls; a re-purposed hospital where a killer baby, freshly born, has murdered all the doctors. Raphaël, now ten, has never seen a horror movie, and says that even if he was old enough, he'd be too scared. But he loves the gory props: severed heads, spray-containers of glutinous blood, horror contact lenses, and the mangled latex ear he is given as a parting gift. When he isn't on set or with his tutor, we play poker with the other cast and crew or wander around Sofia eating street food and visiting churches filled with icons, incense and ethereal chanting. We hang out in bowling alleys, buy rose-petal jam and ultra-realistic plastic ammo in street markets, and haggle for knock-off Zippo lighters in underpasses. A cereal commercial follows, and then a short film in which he plays a religious zealot teenager with a foul-mouthed grandfather. His performance wins him two awards – but it's to be his last film. School, gymnastics, skateboarding and parkour have taken over, and he's maturing into a new phase, moving with the confidence and magnetism that he will carry into adulthood. In his twenties, with that adulthood still new, he's testing his limits, making mistakes and learning from them, and planning the next chapter in his life: a series of documentaries, the expansion of the Wildwork, a Masters degree in environmental conservation, and more activism.

It has barely started when he dies.

CHAPTER 5: WILL YOUR BASELINE SHIFT?

It was in 2019 that Saharan storms first sent clouds of dust blowing 2,000 miles to southern England, where it fell as blood rain. For a couple of weeks that hot April, London wore a coat of gritty red. The desert dust, combined with wind-borne ammonia-based fertiliser and local discharges from traffic and industry, caused a spike in air pollution. But the main topic of discussion during those uncanny days was not the dull, everyday fact of an overheating world – we'd come to live with that – but the freakishness of the red grit. Of the choked, pinkish sky. Of trees, roads, cars and buildings coated in granules.

Shifting baseline syndrome describes how what appears as weird and uncanny on its first appearance becomes first assimilated, then taken as a given. Soon, with the desertification spreading in southern Europe, blood rain and pink dust will be such a common sight that it will be perceived as an ordinary phenomenon. Integrated into our general perception of how weather manifests, it will become normalised. I begin to wonder when my own baseline will shift. Will I stop seeing the surrealness of outliving my son as a seismic horror and assimilate it as a plain, everyday fact of my life? My new normal?

Grief acted on us like concussion. It pulled our faces into unfamiliar configurations, making us strangers to ourselves. In the villa, we put on fresh clothes, washed our hair and brushed our teeth the way we always had – the thing called *keeping it together* – but while our muscle memories were intact, our cognition was in chaos. We were confused about the date and the day of the week. We forgot the name of the woman who'd be coming to help us with the death arrangements. We mislaid mobiles, bags, keys, jackets and laptops. Matti was smoking too much. Michel was driven to distraction by the mystery of Raph's death. And I'd become my own torture chamber. All I wanted was to leave my own skin and swap places with someone else – anybody – if even for a minute. It was as if my body – the body that birthed him – was in the process of a horrific reverse pregnancy, and my son was dissolving inside me, cell by cell.

Yet through all of this, he still felt vividly present and

vibrantly alive – as though *recently dead* somehow meant *still partly living*. To maintain our sense of that vividness, our memories of him, old and recent, took on the cast of precious currency. We exchanged 'classic Raph' moments: Raphaël at nine, cartwheeling the half mile from the station to his father's house; Raphaël at fourteen, winning the heart of a Danish girl two heads taller than him and two years older; Raphaël at twenty, hurling himself off a bridge into the Thames.

We are all naturally argumentative people with firm views, but now, drained of energy, whichever one of us expressed an opinion or made a practical suggestion had the immediate backing of the others. Gallows humour became our preferred means of communication. We joked that we shared a single brain cell that we took turns to use.

'Who's in charge of the brain cell at the moment?' we'd ask each other when a decision was needed. Comedy was the wild card that kept playing itself. Its brief flashes indicated that, despite our madness, we were still partially sane. We didn't feel guilty when something made us laugh or smile. It felt Raph-approved, and positive.

But our bodies were rebelling. Michel had lost his voice. He spoke in a hoarse whisper. I could barely hear him. This was compounded by the low-level ear infection I'd had for weeks: my ears were full of ectoplasm. I wanted to press the volume on a remote control to make Michel speak up. Instead, I bent my ear into a cone shape. Meanwhile Matti had stopped using his contact lenses and reverted to glasses. They were like a shield, he said. When he wanted to disconnect, he could just take them off and be semi-blind. We were the three monkeys, we joked bleakly.

At various times of day, we retreated to phone our partners in Los Angeles, Munich and London, and we'd overhear one another's voices murmuring updates in Danish, Spanish and Italian. Carsten, Piluca and Lara were our missing, essential people: our tethers to the world we'd left behind. We ached for them, but there was no point in their joining us here: with no clear timeline in sight, why get them to come all this way when we'd be needing every ounce of their energy on our return? Instead, we agreed we'd all meet in London for the next milestone of our grotesque family journey.

In the meantime, the immediate future was full of words that made me feel physically sick. Mortuary. Autopsy. Death certificate. Coffin. We'd need to hold a ceremony for family and friends after we arrived in London. The logistics of this were beyond us. But we agreed on one thing. Whatever shape it took, there was one thing we'd never call it − a funeral.

In the midst of this, I scanned the fresh messages of

shock and condolence that avalanched in. I answered as many as I could – often with all I could summon, which was a heart emoji – because they buoyed me up. I was becoming a validation junkie. But it was an untrustworthy fix. I needed to know that other people were traumatised, and shocked, and cared, and couldn't believe it either. An old acquaintance, Thomas, wrote from Denmark. His daughter had been killed in a road accident nine months before. Sorrowfully, he welcomed me to 'the club you didn't ask to join and that you can never leave'. The one that never seeks new members.

The Terrible Club, I thought. I'll call it that.

Over dinner we drank and reminisced about Raph's pre-teen bedroom: an Aladdin's cave of old Heelys and Pokémon cards, bric-a-brac from British car-boot sales and French *brocantes*, and a gigantic ramshackle cage with interconnecting plastic tunnels where his gerbils lived. About how he taught himself to make chain mail, which he made from copper wire, stripped down from flex he fished out of dumpsters. Beneath his desk was a cardboard box of tangled wire thread. He had tweezers, scissors, pincers. An array of goth bling. A Dementor figure with an empty hood. A glass-studded skull. And later, a bucket list. Many of the backpacker hostels he stayed in on his travels had a chalkboard for bucket lists. He took his seriously from the start, filming himself crossing off the items with a pen and a ruler as each was achieved. Among them:

'Touch a tiger and survive.'

'Learn to fly without wings.'

'Have an NDE.'

A Near-Death Experience.

Why was death itself on his bucket list? Oh, Raph. Be normal.

When our shared brain cell was in my custody, I played an online word game obsessively and followed the world news. I couldn't explain it, but it seemed to anchor me. Antarctica had logged its hottest temperature on record: 18.3 degrees Celsius. The American president had fired two officials who gave key testimony in his impeachment inquiry. China had reported eighty-six more deaths from coronavirus, bringing the total to 700. And one of the child stars in *Nanny McPhee* was dead.

'He's going to be remembered for everything,' the activist at XR's London office told me. 'Not just his acting. We'll make sure of it.' They were planning a tribute procession through the streets of London in the next few days. There would be speeches. Singing. Flags. Drums. A celebration of his life. 'Is there anything you think he'd have wanted us to do?' she asked. Remembering the effect it had had on anyone who saw it, I knew immediately. 'Yes. He wants you to screen his dance.'

I realised that throughout our conversation I'd been speaking about Raphaël in the present tense, as if he were alive but temporarily unavailable, and I was his P.A. *Fox likes this, he doesn't like that. Fox wants you to serve flapjacks because they were his speciality. Fox wants you to screen his dance to cheer everyone up. Fox wants you all to dance, too.*

In 2016, when he was hanging out with free-runners in Bangkok, he discovered a deserted shopping mall some-where on the outskirts of the city. Like me, he felt the magnetic pull of built spaces left to crumble, rot and be colonised by wilderness. The dance is wild, inventive and graceful – and, typically of Raph, it includes a terrifying sequence in which he walks across the abyss of a lift shaft on a steel girder. He spent hours editing it. 'One man, one camera, one tripod, two mornings, six hours, no budget,' he wrote afterwards. 'The shoot left me bruised, exhausted, covered in dirt and grime, bleeding in several places, and so freaking satisfied.' But when he posted the film anonymously on YouTube, it attracted barely any views.

'It's like a baby sea-turtle,' he told me, when I asked why he'd done nothing to promote it. 'When they hatch, they scuttle to the sea. Some make it, some don't.'

'We'll screen the dance,' she said.

'Good,' I told her. 'He'll love that.'

As the rain began to pour outside, Matti, Michel and

I watched it on my laptop. There was a sequence I'd forgotten. He's lying on the floor, his hand over his heart, miming a cardiac arrest. We all drew in a sharp breath. Four years ago, he'd performed and filmed a preview of his own death. He's self-defibrillating.

CHAPTER 6: WILL YOU LIVE THROUGH THE WORST DAY?

The sun blazed outside, filling the air with sharp, organic scents I didn't recognise. Matti stood smoking on the veranda. He looked lonely and bewildered and his eyes were red from crying. I willed the long-tailed bird to come back and do a dance that was just for him. But the trees were empty. I went out and hugged him. If Raphaël were here, he'd be the one hugging him. And he'd be saying he was sorry: sorry his brother was suddenly an only child, sorry he'd have to see him in a morgue, sorry he died so young and so far away, sorry he died at all. It wasn't his plan. And then he'd make a joke and make Matti laugh. There was never any doubting they were brothers, but it was when they laughed that the resemblance was at its clearest. They had the same muscular physiques, the same gestures, the same complexions, the same workmanlike hands, the same thick-lashed blue eyes, the same strong eyebrows, the same deep, firm voices. But when they laughed together, flinging back their heads, rocking back and forth, clutching furniture and clasping their bellies, tears pouring from their eyes, they laughed like I have never seen any two people laugh together. In those moments, they were twins.

There was a knock at the door.

Debby ran a local voluntary organisation for trauma victims, and she was here to help us with the arrangements for the autopsy and whatever was to happen next. I hadn't realised how much I had missed being around women. I'd held myself together around all the men we'd met, but as soon as she hugged me I collapsed in tears. The course director would have come too, Debby told us when I'd finished crying, but his baby had just been born. When she handed me her phone, she must have known it's impossible to look at an image of a newborn baby and its happy parents without smiling. The baby was biracial, like the boys' French cousins. In a country traumatised by centuries of racial injustice, it felt like an unexpected gift.

Debby made a point of speaking to us slowly, like we were children learning something new. No stranger to emergencies, she scanned our faces as a doctor might, assessing our ability to understand. When she spoke, her terrible gentleness made me realise this was actually happening. He really was dead.

'You're in shock,' she said, then paused to make sure it was sinking in. 'That's going to last for a while. Don't fight it. You can't. It's doing what it needs to.'

She ran through the classic symptoms of post-trauma, all of which we had experienced: a dry mouth, physical disorientation, memory loss, physical restlessness.

'It's because you don't want to be in your own skin,' she said. 'You're trying to get away from being you.'

Matti and I glanced at each other, pierced by the truth of it.

Debby took a breath, then asked if we have thought of 'having the remains repatriated'.

When we realised what she was asking, we immediately agreed that Raphaël didn't want his corpse flown to the UK like a piece of cargo any more than we did. We'd cremate him here and take his ashes with us. Again, I found myself certain, *It's what Raphaël wants* – as if being dead hadn't stopped him holding firm opinions, and some lingering residue of him was demanding agency.

Alongside helping trauma victims, Debby ran a non-profit organisation focusing on intelligence and analysis to combat the local poaching industry: the world Raphaël was planning to investigate in his documentary. Like all multi-million-dollar industries, it's highly organised, she told us. At the bottom of the five-tier pyramid people risk their lives. The local poachers, usually men, have turned to poaching because they're desperate to feed their families. At the top of the pyramid are international criminals. The two are connected by a series of middlemen who work in what are effectively very loosely structured cells. The endangered animals – rhino, elephant, giraffe and other species – are targeted and identified and the whereabouts of a potential target animal sent to a local organiser who tells a poaching group where to go. A separate chain of command supplies the weapon. Every week, planes and cargo ships leave Eastern Africa loaded with containers bound for countries hungry for smuggled animal parts. Debby's knowledge had been widely used in TV research. She was showing us a photo of her with David Attenborough on her phone when a text came in. She read it, frowning.

'No news on when they'll do the autopsy. It'll be in a few days if you're lucky. If not, it could be another week. I'm sorry. There are a lot of premature deaths here that need investigating.' Accidents. Suicides. Murders.

Raph's body had joined a queue.

When the day comes, I wake feeling nauseous, the dread welling up in me like vomit. I long to see him, but not in this grotesque, perverted way.

I don't want to get in the car. Everything in me resists the overwhelming wrongness of what must now happen. But I have to. Hating it, hating it, hating it, I get in, and Debby drives us through a lush green landscape of acacia trees, mango trees, citrus trees, Death Trees. Slowly, clouds begin to stack in the sky, stark as geological strata. The land is studded by teetering columns and extravagantly fungal mounds as red as the earth they rise from. The edifices could be rock formations, but they are sun-baked mud. Above and below ground, termites are constructing intricate metropolises. Crossing the gushing Olifants river that feeds into the Limpopo, we're struck by its surreal colour. It's not green or blue or silver, but an unnatural, muddy brown. This is largely due to mining, Debby tells us: when the poisonous debris in the water is at its most potent, it hardens the fat of the river's fish and crocodiles. Unable to move, they starve and die.

Debby has warned us that the hospital is poor and run-down. It's a set of grey concrete buildings and outhouses surrounded by a high fence, and the security checks are tight to prevent the theft of dead bodies and babies for use in witchcraft practices: a grisly reminder that it's not just animal parts that can be traded in the name of fear and belief. We stop at a car park and sit in a waiting room under posters about flu, malaria and cholera. The receptionist pointedly ignores us and chats on his mobile. If you work in a morgue, it's just a job. The pathologist hasn't arrived. Nobody knows when she will, and the receptionist tells us there's no guarantee she will let us see Raphaël. Michel has anticipated this, and he is wearing a smart suit – not only because he hopes it will get us all into the morgue, but because if she has to open up Raph's body, he wants to be present. Matti and I think this is a terrible, dangerous idea, but Michel is as stubborn as Raph, so we don't argue. He's doing what he needs to.

Desperate to escape the uncertainty and stress of the waiting room and breathe fresh air, Matti and I move to the fenced semi-wilderness outside. But we bring the tension with us. We don't know where to put ourselves. Matti smokes and grinds his stubs into the car park's cracked cement. It rains sporadically, the drops bouncing off tall feathery grasses. We wander about aimlessly, spiralling first one way then another, then stop and watch some red ants transport a seed towards a tussock. They are diligent and single-minded and full of animal purpose and we are none of these things. We are lost and full of dread. When Michel comes out, we know from the look on his face what that means. We've got permission to see Raphaël's body. Back indoors, the receptionist gestures at a shabby door and says, 'In there.' We take a deep breath and open it, then follow the corridor.

The morgue is dark and refrigerated and smells sharply of disinfectant. There are four or five trolleys with corpses on them, in plastic body-bags: human-shaped grubs in translucent cocoons. Michel points to one at the far end of the room and says, 'That's him.' My heart jumps. *He's wrong. There's been a mistake. He's not that tall.*

But the wishful thought collapses as we approach. The bunched ends of the body-bag make him look longer, that's all. Part of the plastic has been pulled back to expose his head and part of his chest.

It's him.

His shaven head is tilted to the left as if in sleep, away from us.

His skin is pale, mottled in places. His freckles stand out. From his strong, proud nose, there is a line of dried blood.

He's beautiful.

I stay long enough for the image to sear itself on my brain. Long enough to register that the corpse isn't him, but the shell he left behind. He's long gone. I bolt out through the double doors into the open air and stand on a broken concrete threshold surrounded by weeds and grasses and take deep breaths of humid rain-filled air and howl.

Michel and Matti emerge a few minutes later, and we gather in a hug and cry. Afterwards they tell me that they kissed his face. I hadn't thought of doing this. Did Raphaël mind that I couldn't stay as long as they did?

'It was horrible,' says Matti. 'He was cold.'

But not cold enough, we will soon learn. Due to widespread power cuts over the past days, his organs have partly disintegrated, complicating the autopsy – and its results.

Waiting for the pathologist to begin the autopsy, we go out again and pace around beneath an overcast sky, near a car park with a van marked 'Limpopo Province Forensic Pathology Services'. It's for transporting corpses, organs, specimens. Warm rain begins to spatter down. I want it to dissolve me and let me quietly cease. This will forever be the worst day of my life.

It's night-time in LA and I don't want to wake Carsten, so I call my friends Polly and Sandy. Their voices are full of love and understanding. There's nothing to say but I say it anyway, and they say it back, and I sob. When Matti finishes his call to his girlfriend Piluca, we knuckle away our tears and meander in widening circles, aware of the truth of what Debby told us: that we are moving around to escape our own skins.

After a while, the message comes from the pathologist: having opened the chest cavity, she can confirm that it's neither thrombosis nor pneumothorax, and the toxicity report is clear. It's definitely not a snakebite. In fact, there's still no visible, clear-cut cause of death. Michel is stricken.

He knows exactly what this means. The pathologist will have to open him up further. And he must witness it. We implore him not to put himself through it, but know we can't stop him. It's the longest fifteen minutes of our lives. He never tells us what he sees on the autopsy table, and we never ask. But he leaves the building almost at a run. We run after him and when we catch up with him along the side of the building he half collapses, and he's crying so hard we have to hold him upright. I have never seen such brokenness in another human.

'I had to do it,' he keeps saying through his tears. 'I had to do it for Raph.'

Two and a half hours later the pathologist calls us in. She is young, pretty, serious and heavily pregnant. After so long on her feet she is clearly exhausted. Raphaël's lungs are far too big, she tells us. And so is the right ventricle of his heart. She will send samples to the lab, which is in another district. But she warns that we can't expect much, given the disintegration of his organs. We don't know this yet, but it will take Michel months of dogged work to track down the lab results, and the samples will remain in limbo for four and a half years. We take the temporary death certificate – a flimsy piece of paper, hand-written, with the cause of death named as 'Right ventricular hypertrophy due to pulmonary stenosis'. There it is, in black and white. We saw his body and now we've got the paperwork. He's dead, and here's the proof. The pathologist tells us they'll issue a formal death certificate later and send us the lab results. But they never do.

Back outside, we wait until a trolley emerges bearing an ochre body-bag that looks vaguely ecclesiastical and closes with a zip. This time there's no doubting it's him. I've seen him like this often, in sleeping bags. Unable to watch while they manoeuvre him into the crematorium estate car, I turn away, but when they get ready to drive off, I'm distraught. Before he leaves, I want him to know I'm sorry I let him down. I should have stayed longer with him, and kissed his face like the others did. But I couldn't. I ran away. What kind of mother runs away from her son's dead body? I torment myself with the thought for a while until I finally accept defeat and sit silently in the back of the car.

On the drive back we travel on a long straight road between two fenced-off territories. Debby tells us the one on the left is a nature reserve where the wildlife is protected, and the other is a game farm where animals are bred for the wildlife industry, and hunters shoot game for trophies. On the anti-poaching course that Raphaël was on, some of the students would go on to work on nature reserves. Others would work on game farms, where their job would be to prevent poachers illegally killing wild animals, so that testosterone-crazed trophy-hunters could do it themselves, with the blessing of the law. I note the hypocrisy and the injustice of such a system, but it doesn't enrage me. Right now, in my numbed state, it feels no more or less grotesque than what we are living through. Just a plain, ugly fact that must be absorbed.

Behind the fence of the nature reserve stand four elephants. One is small, a baby. Suddenly, Michel asks Debby to stop the car.

'He sent us a sign!' he says, in tears.

I'm surprised. This is not like Michel. But none of us are who we were. I saw the red-tailed bird do its dance. And now it's his turn. The elephants appeared when he needed them, and now we have both become the people who have existed throughout history: the parents who have lost a child and are suddenly open to signs.

That night, watching the clips from the XR tribute to Iggy Fox in London through my tears, I could see that the vigil was astonishing: hundreds of people walking with bowed heads, flanked by police, and led by XR co-founder Simon Bramwell, my brother Tom, and Raph's cousin Anna. Mourners speak about Iggy Fox's charisma, his compassion, his bravery, his ingenuity, his dedication to the cause – and their desolation at his loss. Among them are indigenous

Brazilians from the Amazon, bearing images of him, and others who never knew him but want to honour him. There are poems and speeches and a haunting Shetland dirge, its notes called out and echoed by the crowd, thumping their chests in a heartbeat rhythm as the procession moves into Trafalgar Square. There, a vast silk flag billows and dances in the dark night to the sound of a poem and a song by his friend Blythe, with the crowd on harmonies. Later, outside Parliament, he gets his wish. On a giant scaffold screen on the side of Westminster Abbey, he comes alive. And dances.

He'd have loved that. Oh, how he'd have loved it.

At the crematorium, we asked to see him one last time. Not his face or body: just his hand. His left forearm, decorated with a sleeve tattoo of a jaguar, emerged from the cocoon of the upholstered body-bag. His thumbnail was dark purple. His freckles stood out against the paleness of his skin.

We were all crying. I touched his hand, then kissed it. It was very cold, like meat from a fridge. I don't need to tell you that it was unbearable.

Then we watched a man in a boilersuit shunt the chipboard box into the furnace with a mechanised shovel system. It was like watching a pizza entering a hot oven. He closed the iron door, bolted it with a clang and waited for our signal. Whoever had the brain cell must have nodded, because he pulled a lever and the machine ground into motion. And we stood and watched our astonishing boy go up in smoke, until we could watch no more.

There were no birds in the sky, and no clouds. Just his ashes, and the sun, and his atoms, and the light. Energy doesn't disappear, it transforms. He was energy now. Pure, invisible, disembodied energy. I longed for a way to reach out to that energy, and connect with it. But how?

That night, as I took a sleeping pill, I had the thought that he might come to me in a dream. But I slept like the dead. The next morning we returned to the crematorium to collect the ashes and sign papers and cry more hot, violent tears. We'd dealt with this. We'd risen to the occasion. But a vital part of each of us was gone.

CHAPTER 7: WILL YOU DANCE?

In South Africa, my heart had physically ached. That pain was acute. But now, in London, it was setting up home, and becoming chronic. It felt as if a mineral had accreted in there, forming ugly, jagged crystals. It was blood temperature and a muddy dark purple. Mostly it just sat motionless, but occasionally it shifted its weight and tortured me in a new place. The urgent need to not be me rooted itself deeper. But I was stuck with who I was.

Grief is a besiegement of the body, but it also hijacks the mind. Mine was faltering and stalling, a jumble of meat and synapses and stories. In mathematics, chaos theory describes apparently random or unpredictable behaviour within systems that are governed by deterministic laws. A more accurate term is 'deterministic chaos', because in connecting two notions that are familiar and commonly regarded as incompatible, a paradox is implied. Familiar but incompatible – my son is dead.

Even as we prepared for what we were now calling a memorial, the urge to deny Raphaël's death – to somehow *cancel* it – appealed to me. I have a good imagination: I knew if I made a superhuman effort, I could do it. In a hyper-connected age in which parents expect instant access to their children at all times, I never had that luxury with Raphaël. When he was working on conservation projects, off the grid, I often wouldn't hear from him for a month or two. So now it would be no great stretch to convince myself he was overseas in a remote camp, shaving his stubble with a machete, mending a broken roof, photo-graphing the claw-marks of big cats, cooking jungle stew, watching a spider methodically spin its web.

There were so many other ways he could have died, many of them stupid. On the day he was born, the hospital didn't have a bed for me, so I was left in the delivery room. After a while I needed to pee, so, clutching Raphaël to my chest, I manoeuvred us off the trolley – and my legs gave way. I fell, hard, and came close to dropping him on the tiled floor. I'd had an epidural, which hadn't worked when I was giving birth. But now it had. No one thought to warn me.

Then there were the many times he risked splitting his

head open doing urban gymnastics with his parkour mates, the many times he got drunk, the many times he took hallucinogenic drugs, the many times he handled dangerous animals, the time his lung collapsed, the time he was so sick they had to give him an IV drip halfway up a mountain, the time he caught dengue fever.

I knew his fieldwork was always going to be dangerous, but when he began studying venomous snakes I made a vow to him and to myself: no more worrying. It doesn't help. I have a son who leads a risky life and always will. So if something was to happen, I'd cross that bridge when I came to it. And now I'd come to it.

In my dream, Matti, Michel and I get a message that Raph has been moved to a hospital ward with other patients and their families, and we are allowed to visit him. He isn't alive, we're told, *but he isn't dead either.* We are confounded, but excited. How can it be possible? But it is. He's propped up on a high bed, shaven-headed and bruised. He isn't conscious but his body's moving. He is the corpse I saw in the morgue, but with blood and breath and a pumping heart. He has no cognitive faculties. But he can move his limbs, and his head, and he can grunt and sigh.

We celebrate. We got him back! An older woman tending her daughter in a nearby bed leans across conspiratorially. We are the lucky families, she conveys to us. There aren't many who come back like this. It's very rare. We are jubilant that he is showing signs of life, even if he can't speak, even if he stumbles around blind, like the other patients, and is clearly a vegetable. We stroke his cold skin and tell him we love him. We tell him everything's OK, he's alive, and he's with his family, and that's all that matters. As I started to wake, I clung on to the dream, not wanting it to fade. I wanted to stay in the place where his body moved again, and where I settled, happily, for a zombie son.

But as the day dawned, so did reality. There were arrangements to be made for the final goodbye in London. *Power to the Mama*, Raph used to sing on Women's Day marches, in his joke opera baritone. *Mama got the power*. But Mama was a wreck. And she had no power. Fortunately, others did. The Akan proverb *owuo atwedee baakofoo mforo* translates as 'death's ladder is not climbed by only one person'. And we were many. Michel's partner welcomed me into the home that was once mine, long ago. Raphaël often said he loved her, and I knew she loved him back. Wordlessly, we broke into tears and hugged. Working in miserable solidarity, Matti and Raph's friends from the Wildwork and Extinction Rebellion took over all the practicalities. They found a beautiful, light-filled venue in Kew Gardens, its walls decorated with prints of plants and flowers. They tracked people down, drew up the guest list, found a vegetarian caterer, and sent out invitations with an image painted by a friend: a fox with an eyebrow piercing just like Raph's. Everything was ready. But when the time came, when all I needed to do was show up, Carsten had to almost frog-march me to the taxi. I was the dog that senses danger and baulks, snarling. On the way to Kew Gardens, I felt nothing but a dark, deep, sickening dread.

Half an hour later, 130 people were arriving, most of them his friends and peers. Raph's partners Kira and Savannah cried in one another's arms. We didn't bring the ashes and hardly anyone wore black because this wasn't a funeral, and we'd never call it one. We wouldn't just mourn his death. We were there to celebrate his life. The older generations arrived first and spoke quietly in small groups, exchanging condolences and memories of Raphaël. For a while, it felt surreally sedate. But soon we were outnumbered by young people, and the big hall teemed with activists, childhood friends, schoolmates, conservationists, actors, parkourists, filmmakers, friends, colleagues and lovers. And as the alcohol flowed, the atmosphere became charged with something wild and fresh and utterly unfiltered. Young grief doesn't hold back. Young grief howls and chokes and growls and wails. Young grief group-hugs and wears jewellery made by Raph, and drinks hard and fast and goes outside to smoke and breakdance and turn somersaults on the darkening lawn.

On the stage stands a huge photo of Raphaël in the Bolivian jungle with a male red howler monkey perched on his shoulder, like a father with his child. In his speech, Michel talks about how the monkey's fur is exactly the same russet as Raph's hair, so it's impossible to see where the human ends and the animal begins, which is a good metaphor for his life, because he saw us all as creatures. Raph's closest university friends talk about how he believed in them sometimes even more than they believed in themselves, and they became who they are because of him. His parkour mate Femi gives a funny, heart-rending speech about their teenage years scoping out stairwells, jumping across concrete chasms, running and somer-saulting through the urban wild. His half-sister Lydia speaks of their happy, nerdy kinship, and two of Raph's child co-stars read a warm, wise speech sent by Emma Thompson, and there are songs from Raph's French cousin Anna and two of his friends, and through the blur of my tears it comes to me that there are so many different Raphaëls, all filtered through the prism of each unique relationship. But today all of them are here.

Then comes Raphaël's moment. Kirk Jones, the director of *Nanny McPhee*, has put together a beautiful short film. The images are stills of Raph, and Kirk's footage of Extinction Rebellion's recent tribute to him on the streets of London, and the words are from 'Why I Rebel',

Raphaël's hymn to activism. As a last gift to his brother, Matti voices them.

Science alone is silence. For people to act on science's warnings and apply its solutions, its message needs shouting from the rooftops. Scientists are getting on the streets, refusing to be scribes of the apocalypse.

After seven years studying, researching and protecting nature as a wildlife conservationist, I stopped fieldwork and deferred an MSc in order to rebel full-time. Because no matter how many surveys I ran, how many turtle nests I protected, or how many young people I educated about 'sustainability', the seas kept rising, forests kept burning, plastic kept clogging the beaches, and our data kept showing that wildlife was being decimated.

On August 13th, six of us were arrested at London's Brazilian Embassy for taking non-violent direct action to highlight an ecological and human rights emergency. We did it as two thousand Indigenous women marched on Brasilia to defend their lives and lands, and three days after the Dias do Fogo, when thousands of fires were lit to clear deforested land in the Amazon.

I don't want to go to prison, but I'll face whatever I have to. My actions aren't about sacrifice, or arrest for the sake of it. Knowing the science, I have no choice but to tell the truth, and stick to my morals in the face of that truth. I won't stand by and watch the world burn.

The film ends in Trafalgar Square, with Raph's dance being projected onto a huge screen in front of Westminster Abbey, across from Parliament, and the crowd fox-howling up into the winter night. My heart is breaking all over again. How can someone so full of life be dead?

I haven't been sure I'll be capable of giving the eulogy I've prepared, so my childhood friend Jo is standing by to take over if I can't. But seeing the film and hearing Matti reading his brother's words have given me a shot of energy. I can do this much for Raph. And I will, because I want him to feel proud of me. And I'll regret it if I don't. I take a deep breath and pick up the microphone, and read the words I wrote on the aeroplane from Texas to Dubai with more confidence than I knew was in me, because I feel his strength. 'Raph, you are a force of nature, and now you are one with that force. You are water, you are chlorophyll, you are moss on a stone, a bird's feather, a wolf's paw print, an oak tree, a praying mantis, a stingray, a garden squirrel. You are the sky and the sea and the rainforests and the mountains and the marshes and the deserts and all the landscapes you ever knew and loved. You were a joyous, crazy gift to all of us.'

I'm speaking with my own voice, but I speak as I hope he'd want me to speak. I speak in the hope that I can be more like him. I speak in the knowledge that he's alive as long as his name is spoken and his life remembered – and beyond. And then we show his dance.

It's sunrise in Bangkok. As the music creeps in and builds, he lowers himself through a hole in the roof of a crumbling shopping mall. He dangles for a moment, then drops. He drops again. And again. And again. Landing near a broken lift shaft beneath the open sky, he walks down a mossy escalator, then leaps off it sideways. Stripping off his hoodie, he puts on a pair of dirty old trainers, dodges a flitting bird, tests his shoes on the blistered concrete, pacing out the space. Then a sideways shuffle, and he's facing the camera, a mask over his face, headphones over his ears, and a thick strap on his left bicep. His muscular bare arms are level with his heart, one forearm resting on the other. Then his linked hands begin sketching rapid, fluid shapes, his feet kicking restlessly at the floor – and with a swift spin his hands are at his chest again. Blink and you'd miss it, but he's made the shape of a heart. And now his whole body is a whirl of movement, robotic jerks morphing into a cooler, seamless flow. He swivels and launches into a half-cartwheel, and then he's a whirling man-bird in semi-flight, kicking away broken cement as his limbs move faster and faster. And then he falls.

He falls again.

He falls again.

He falls again.

He falls a final time but this time he stays down. He's on his back, outstretched, exhausted, his right hand over his heart. His chest is heaving. He's fighting for air. His heart is failing, and he is making the jerky movements of a young man dying of a heart attack. Everyone draws in a breath at that moment. The moment he pre-enacts his death.

How did you know, Raph? Did you feel it in your cells? Did you see it in a dream, or was it an intuition, like mine from years ago? How can we have known something that it's scientifically impossible to know?

Then he bounces up and he's whirling again, ecstatically resurrected, and the video plays again, and the whole room is on its feet, and we dance our grief, we dance our love of him, we dance our bewilderment, we dance the wrongness of it, we dance the rise and fall of aeons and ecosystems, we dance the spinning galaxies, we dance our agony at the loss of his radiance, we dance his resurrection, we dance to stay alive and we dance to keep him with us, always.

PART TWO: SPRING

CHAPTER 8: WILL YOU ENTER
A COCOON?

In our apartment in Copenhagen, a dank, mournful chaos prevails. A pipe has burst in the attic above our living room, so there's the rumble of dehumidifiers and a damp miasma permeates every room. As the hours bleed into one another, I fantasise about falling asleep for five years and waking to find the pain has softened – yet every day that pulls me further from Raphaël's living presence is another wound. And now, suddenly, death is everywhere.

Kairos has struck again, and within the space of days 2020 has become a year that no one will forget. We are already cocooned in grief, but with lockdown as the new backdrop to our private misery we become doubly absent from the world. Carsten is now my sole horizon and I am his. We cry together and we cry separately. Whenever one of us mentions Raphaël and bursts into tears, the other does too. Secretly, I feel it's quite appropriate that with my son dead the entire world should stop in its tracks and ask the same questions I've been asking: How did this happen? What am I supposed to do? How long will the pain last? Can I learn to live differently, and if so, how? Can something positive emerge from anything this brutal?

Raph would see the pandemic as an opportunity. Just look at how nations have mobilised on a massive scale and raised vast sums of money to counter this, he'd say. And look at how people are willing to drastically alter their lives to stay safe. If that kind of energy can be summoned to tackle this, it can be summoned to combat a far bigger and more lethal threat. And even if all the obvious lessons are ignored, it's proof that drastic swerves are possible. Framing it that way, as the weeks go by I take heart in the fact that people are noticing and appreciating the sound of birdsong, the cleaner air and the plane-free skies. In this window of time that scientists have dubbed the 'anthropause', flowers grow through pavement cracks, Punjabis can see the Himalayas for the first time in decades, and wildlife is claiming new space: I watch clips of goats and deer strolling down suburban British streets, kangaroos bounding through the empty streets of Adelaide, penguins crossing streets in Cape Town.

But another part of me is queasily aware that as the virus spreads, so does the death count and the map of grief. Every day there are freshly bereaved parents, new orphans, widowers and widows reeling from the sudden absence of a loved one who died too soon. *Orphan, widow, widower.* In Arabic, a bereaved father is a *thakil* and a bereaved mother is a *thakla.* In Hebrew it's *shakul* and *shakula.* In Mandarin, if your only child has died you are a *shidu.* Why is there no word in English for a parent whose child has died? Is it too unspeakable? As the situation worsens, my anxiety deepens. Might I become a widow as well as a *thakla* or a *shakula?* Carsten's history of asthma makes him vulnerable to the virus.

'You can't die too,' I tell him. I mean it more than he knows. We have loved each other for almost twenty years and I refuse to lose him. He's used to seeing me in tears – but now I'm icily strategic. I can see it shocks him, but I don't care. From now on, I announce, I will shop and he will cook. There will be no dispute, because it's a unilateral decision. He can go for walks alone, or with me or his daughter Laura. But beyond that he's imprisoned – and I'm his gaoler. I buy sanitiser and masks.

Laura is our only regular visitor, and Raphaël's death has hit her hard. She'll never laugh with him again, tease him and be teased, take him out dancing with her friends or exchange eye-rolls when Carsten or I say something ridiculous. The last time he was in Copenhagen she didn't get to say a proper goodbye. None of us did.

It was a December night, and twenty young activists were crammed into our apartment. The American glaciologist Jason Box was our guest of honour: he spoke about his task of charting the acceleration of the Greenland ice-cap's disappearance, and the blindness of world governments to its significance. Raphaël and his partner Kira had been staying with us after taking part in a mass anti-coal protest in Germany where they'd clashed with police: they had scarred their fingertips using a razor and superglue to avoid a fingerprint record, and Raph's hand was swollen from a truncheon attack. He and I always loved to cook and serve food together, and we'd made vegan pizzas. But soon after we'd eaten, he and Kira had to rush off to catch their coach. Raphaël had pasted a fabric sign on our door, which he'd stencilled himself: the XR hour-glass symbol on a sky-blue background, and the words ACT NOW. As they left, he was about to take it with him, then changed his mind. 'Keep it,' he said. 'I'll make some more.'

As the weeks pass, his friends and I write to one another, or call, or send heart and fox emojis. I'm grateful that the web of connection is there, but conscious that unless I tend to it, it could dissolve with time. The people who loved Raph will never forget him and will continue to be inspired by him, but they are young people with their lives ahead of them. One of them, a filmmaker who was going to edit Raphaël's documentary, sends me an email. He was looking through the footage they shot for the Crowdfunder just before Fox left for South Africa, and there's something in it I might like to see, he writes. Should he send it? Yes. He should.

I steel myself, take a deep breath and press play. As I feared, it hits me like a gut-punch to see Raphaël so unquestionably alive now that he's so unquestionably dead. He's outdoors, in a wood. He has worked in front of cameras since he was a kid, so he is professional, his voice friendly but serious, his gestures easy and welcoming. But he fluffs a take, and, with the camera still running, he and the filmmaker start to chat about what it might take for the anti-poaching documentary to make an impact.

'I could die,' Raphaël says. Then he laughs at the absurdity of it. 'I'll try not to. I mean, I might get shot. But it's more likely to be snakebite.' Then he smiles and does another take.

I could die.

I watch it again. And again. And again.

Bit apprehensive, he wrote to me in his last message. *I could die*, he told his friend.

Snakebite. There are deadly snakes in South Africa, but

when I look through his notebook I discover another reason snakes were on his mind. One of the last entries, dated the 1st of January, is almost illegible – as if he wrote it half-awake. In the dream, he's been sabotaging a factory. There's a big party afterwards, and press coverage. There's the word 'ambush' and a reference to a fight with two opponents. 'As the fight re-starts,' he writes, 'my bare foot is bitten by an orange snake. I lie down after killing the snake and ask a local what it is. He shakes his head and says it is bad – he estimates I have 200 days to live. I start to cry in hospital. I am thinking what to do with my 200 days.'

On January 1st he had not 200 days, but thirty-seven. When I look up snakebite dreams, I learn they can be interpreted as attempts to get your attention. They can represent fear, danger, healing, wisdom or a shedding of the past. Did the dream shake him up? If it did, why didn't he listen to the warning?

'Raph, that other dream you had when you were little,' I ask him aloud. 'You dreamed you were going to die then too. And you were upset because you couldn't stop me and Papa crying. What did it mean?'

'It meant I did have something incurable,' he answers. 'It meant I was always going to die before both of you.'

Is he saying this because he's actually communicating with me, or because I'm imagining him saying it? I remember that when Michel called to tell me Raphaël had died I told him with utter conviction: 'He was going to die no matter what.' Why did I say that? Was it intuition, based on Raph's prophetic dream, or my deep-rooted fear that I'd one day lose a child? Or was I channelling Raph, whose unconscious mind knew his days were numbered, and days before his death said on camera: *I could die*?

In my dream that night, my calendar has lost some crucial pages. It shows the weeks that have passed – but the future has gone. I've ripped it out, and I must reconstruct it. But then in the dream a question comes to me. *What's the point of planning anything? What's wrong with an empty calendar, in which nothing ever happens?* Time buckles and stretches. Past, present and future are nothing more than stubbornly persistent illusions, according to Einstein. I long for peace. But grief won't let me alone. It shifts violently. It writhes, darkly ruminative, its dark, metallic blood-taste filling all the space I have and demanding more. If there are shots to be called, it's calling them, not me. Yet, much as I loathe it, there are the other times, just as disturbing, when my grief sits strangely motionless and leaves me so numb that I worry that it's dead and that I don't have feelings any more. What sort of mother am I? In these still hours that should feel like grace, or a reprieve, I want my pain back. Urgently. All of it. It's proof that he's alive in me. Because my grief is where he lives.

But perhaps he lives elsewhere too. The pigeon I keep noticing on the balcony is one of several regulars, but unlike the others it has pale brown plumage tinged with pink, and when it alights and eyes the dish of seed I've started leaving out, it fixes me with its unblinking orange eye in a way that makes me think it's noticing me back. Every day it allows me to come a little closer, but never close enough to touch – not that I need to. It's enough to watch the way its glossy neck feathers, the green-mauve of an unripe plum, deepen to purple when it swivels its head. The way it hops along the rail, waiting its turn in the pecking order, and selects the sunflower seeds before the other smaller grains. I appreciate its constancy. And maybe it appreciates mine too. It's a simple thing for a bird and a woman to show up like this for one another every day and look into one another's eyes. Mine see only forward and peripherally, framing the way humans perceive their immediate environment – and time itself. Birds don't have the same understanding of time as we do. But they can see all that's above, below and around, making their presence central, and surrounded by the entire world.

A woman and a bird: a simple daily encounter of two species that feels like much more. Is it a triumph or a tragedy that one modest urban pigeon can make me believe that my son is around me in the form of energy? And that Simone Weil was right to insist that 'what we call super-natural is something science hasn't yet understood'?

'A triumph,' whispers Raphaël.

Of course he does.

The feeling of concussion hasn't lifted. Cognitively impaired, I mislay things, lose track of time, zone out of conversations, stare at nothing. It's my body that sets the agenda now. It wants me either supine on a couch or doing something – anything – with my hands. I re-arrange the glass ornaments that hang from the bicycle-wheel-chandelier I made a year ago, sort out clothes to recycle, scrub at floor stains until my elbows ache. I uproot indoor plants and re-pot them, seized by the need to crumble and sniff a root ball, to plunge my hands in soil and draw muddy, gritty power into myself, as if willing my body to capture and harness the light's energy like chlorophyll does, to put out tendrils and shoots and feel something deep and mythic galvanise my blood, a force that might be courage.

It helps. But it's only outdoors that something truly shifts. Here, in the periphery of my vision, Danish spring is establishing itself. When I feel the rain, wind or sun on my face, I can fleetingly escape the cage of my own head and find the kind of flow that comes not through thoughts, but through the senses. In the fresh air, I become an antenna for small changes in weather and temperature, sensitive to the movements of clouds and birds and the faint mineral tang of the sea.

The guerrilla garden on the corner of our street began as a lone hornbeam tree surrounded by an unloved triangle of poor soil that was used as a toilet by passing dogs. Three years ago, in the absence of a garden of my own, I began planting around the hornbeam, longing for dappled foliage and bright petals; the thrust and dieback of bud and shoot; the complex, shifting odours of organic matter. I wasn't the only one resisting the concrete landscape. Soon the neighbours had joined in, putting in random seeds and corms and bulbs, and when we installed a wooden bench, the corner became a meeting point. In summer it's alive with irises, marigolds, sunflowers, roses, poppies, lavender and visiting insects. Now, neglected all winter, the garden is a chaos of litter and straggly, rotting stalks. Driven by an urge to do something with my hands, I pick out the cigarette butts and the firework squibs from New Year's Eve, clear dead leaves off snowdrops and anemones, check the emerging shoots of daffodils and pull up weeds. The feel of the rough, cold aliveness of soil on my skin frees me from the claustrophobia of my head and gives me blind blood-rush that hints at an escape: a primal sense of belonging to a larger force of energy that lends me its strength when I have none myself. We are creatures. We do what our bodies need.

This is how I can live. And how I can begin to heal.

CHAPTER 9: WILL YOU TEND YOUR GRIEF?

People keep telling me there are no rules for grief, and I agree. But I want wisdom, and I don't know how to get it. I google: *What to do when you lose a child*. Some of the posts and articles that appear are probably wise, and might even help me, but I can't read them. I didn't lose a child. I lost Raphaël, and that isn't something you can google.

So I hunt down podcasts about other people who have endured traumas of all kinds (*What if a murderer appeared at your bedroom door? What if you were seduced into a whole new world? What if you witnessed a horrific act? What if you were entangled in a web of shame?*) and I devour books about death, the afterlife and spirituality with a hunger that feels almost physical, as if I am giving myself a life-saving crash

92

course in survival. Which perhaps I am. I am drawn especially to works by scholars who have lost children of their own, like the grief psychologist David Kessler, who, after the sudden death of his son, added a sixth stage to his colleague Elisabeth Kübler-Ross's stages of grief: meaning. Or the physician Joseph E. Kasper, who expands on the post-traumatic growth concept to introduce the notion of 'co-destiny', a form of mental expansion in the wake of a seismic event that fuses the living parent with their dead child. 'I realised that my destiny was to live my life in a way that would make my son proud,' he writes. Both strike a deep chord in me, and signpost ways ahead that feel possible. But while the field of grief studies has spawned a mass of literature, and I am grateful to all those who strive to help the grieving inspect the fragments of their shattered world-view and build a new one, just go to any cemetery and ask the bereaved what grief system they're using. Who answers 'I'm a Freudian', or 'My grief is Kübler-Rossian', or 'I favour the dual process'? Their grief is simple: *I'm sad. I miss my loved one. I come here to talk to them.*

Books, I soon realise, are not enough. I have vowed to try anything and everything and I need the support of living, breathing people who I can physically meet. So I sign up to a church-organised grief group – the only kind available to me – with my ghost child and my low

93

expectations of Lutheranism in tow. The scent of purple and white lilac fills the streets. The magnolias are opening up like wild candelabras, and, everywhere, life is insisting on fresh growth. But the jarring wrongness of newly burgeoning life unsettles me. It's too much, too soon. And too alive.

The crypt is cold and spacious, with a grand piano, a table of coffee thermoses and a circle of chairs, pulled back to form a socially distanced circle. I feel raw, but I can see I'm not alone. The handful of others in the group are even more recently bereaved than I am, which makes me a kind of veteran. I'm also the only foreigner, and the priest, rightly guessing that I haven't been raised on Danish restraint, suggests I speak first. 'Are you OK with that?'

I glance across at the grand piano, where Raphaël is perched. I knew he'd be here because he's with me more and more. Sometimes he's tiny, like a little hologram, but today I see him life-sized, in ripped jeans and a T-shirt printed with black and grey roses. His wrists are decked in the usual assortment of bands and bracelets, and his long auburn braid – how proud he is of his hair – flipped over his shoulder. *Say yes*, he mouths, and winks. I can sense he finds this new scenario amusing.

I don't particularly want to be the first to offer up my pain to this meeting, but I've promised myself that I won't hold back, whether my experiences are welcome in a church or not. So I begin. I tell them I'm allergic to organised religion, and I certainly didn't believe in an afterlife before Raphaël died. But he's still around. He sends me signs. And he's right here in this room, now. He's pretty much everywhere. I don't care if I sound crazy. As I tell them about my premonition I would lose a child, and Raph's childhood dream, and the bird that danced for me in South Africa, and the pink-brown pigeon, and the film clip, a bereaved husband leans forward nodding enthusiastically. His wife is still around too, he says, and she sends him signs that bring him comfort. While the others take turns to tell their wrenching stories, Raphaël performs a cartwheel on the red-tiled floor, then jumps onto the piano-top and does a handstand. He's learned to do that since he died, apparently.

It's the bereaved husband's turn. As he talks about his wife, I see a woman standing behind him. Either I'm imagining things very vividly today, or she's somehow there in some ghostly form. She isn't tall. She has an instantly likeable, roundish face and a bob of dark-blonde hair and a lovely smile that reveals good, strong teeth. She stands behind her husband and wraps her arms around him as he speaks, and as she kisses the top of his bald head I see the immense and generous nature of their love. They're soulmates. And she is proud of him. I don't want to startle him by claiming I've seen a vision of his dead wife kissing his head. But I decide to write down what I saw, because in a future session we'll be sharing photos and stories of our lost loved ones. If his photo of his wife fits my vision of the woman who kissed his head then I'll show him what I wrote.

A few weeks later, the grief group meets again, this time online, and we show our photos. The bereaved husband shares one of his wife and I hold my breath. It's the woman I saw, without a doubt. When we take a break for coffee, I email him the description I wrote last time we met. And when he writes back, I feel the immediate, deep connection that I have met in activism, and which Raphaël incarnated when he lived, with friends and strangers: the fellowship of something viscerally shared.

My grief rituals have come to me instinctively. Raphaël has no grave, but wanting a place to talk to him I've constructed a makeshift shrine in my writing-room, nested in a set of bookshelves. Its centrepiece is the box containing my third of his ashes and as the weeks pass I add other things, which I like to re-arrange like the contents of a tiny bedroom: his baby-blanket; the carved wooden jewellery box in the shape of a turtle that he gave me at the age of seven; a vulture feather he found in Africa; a jar of pollen from a bee-keeper, which he insisted had magical, energising properties; a lock of his long, wavy auburn hair in a glass container, which I take out to stroke; pictures of him as a baby, and as a boy, and as a man; the block of glass he gave me one Mother's Day when he was ten, engraved with *Mum, I love you*. Next to it, aeons old, is a favourite object of Raphaël's, a tiny time-traveller from the mind-bendingly distant eras that led to this moment: a fossilised fish from the Jurassic era, embedded in a shard of stone. Everything here is sacred.

By five every afternoon, when I feel the storm coming, I don't resist it. I lie on the sofa, clutch the ash-box to my chest, light candles, wrap Raph's baby-blanket round my shoulders and let it do its work. My crying has become fiercer and more desolate since South Africa, as if my cells are recognising that his absence is a fixture. When I feel it blowing in, I surrender to it, and let it crash through me. Carsten has learned that I need to be alone for this, and that there's nothing he can do to comfort me. The crying jags leave me emptied and reeling, but they bring relief. Not just because of the pressure-release, or because crying alleviates distress by activating the parasympathetic nervous system, and releasing oxytocin and endorphins, but because I feel better having spent time with Raphaël. I can't call it quality time. But as it's the only time I'll get, I'll settle for it. And when it has blown through me there is a kind of peace.

'Just breathe,' I heard him say gently once, to someone in distress. 'Take a long slow breath in,' he said, 'and breathe out to the count of four, and then breathe in again. I'll do it with you. One, two, three, four . . .'

And as I breathe, he breathes too, with the lungs I lend him. Or that's how it can seem, on a good day, in those fleeting moments when I am at peace, lifted to somewhere else, floating timelessly in a sunlit spaciousness.

The Danish philosopher Søren Kierkegaard wrote that life must be understood backwards yet lived forwards. When I look backwards, Raphaël's death is meaningless, and I don't have another narrative right now: I only have questions. Maybe what Kierkegaard meant by understanding was actually something more like interpreting, or framing, or simply composing a version of the truth that you can tolerate.

Advice to Self when Questioned about my Children

Learn to give an answer that is dependent on who asks. Choose between the following:

'I have two sons.' (*Applies to people you will not meet again.*)

'I have a son.' (*Also applies to people you will not meet again, but you are unlikely to ever deploy this phrasing as it negates his existence.*)

'I have two sons but one is no longer with us.'

'One of my sons is dead.'

'My younger son died.'

'One of my sons *was* alive, and the other one still is.'

'My younger son died when he was twenty-five. He collapsed and died while out running, probably of an undetected heart defect that caused a fatal electrical misfiring. They call it athlete's heart. Don't ask me any more. Just go away and fucking google it.'

Learn that people mean well, but not everybody deserves to hear the story of his death. Learn to say 'My son died' while secretly thinking: *Raphaël didn't die. He lived.*

But some narratives construct themselves, uncontrollably. I'm already worried about Carsten getting infected, but I have another son: what if I lose him too? A magical thought starts blooming. Because of the pandemic, Matti's heart tests, which should indicate whether he has the same anomaly that probably killed his brother, have been postponed until September. But even if he's clear, something else could kill him. I become irrational. How can I keep him safe if I can't watch him every minute of every day? My ancient fear returns. His hobby is rock–climbing, and in my head he falls. Then he falls again. And falls again. I picture his crushed skull. I picture his broken limbs.

I picture him paralysed from the neck down, breathing through a tube and begging the doctors to let him die. I picture losing him too. Yet I understand his need to climb. Endorphins are the body's medicine, and I know, from the way he talks about it, that his craving for the rockface has taken on a new, more urgent cast: his body needs to tie the knots, to judge the rope's slack, to read the fissures and make the thousand precise calculations the climb demands as he ascends to a place that offers him peace. Even if I wanted to stop him doing it, I couldn't. And why spoil his pleasure by sharing my nightmare scenarios? I can't take his pain away from him, or be there to comfort him. I can't do his grief for him. It's all his own.

I'm thinking about this as I wander from aisle to aisle in the supermarket, picking up and replacing items, terminally indecisive, not knowing what I'm looking for, a consumer who can't even consume efficiently. Places beyond the confines of our home have begun to take on a surreal, dream-like quality. The chilled sections are suddenly not full of meat, but full of chopped-up animals. Chickens. Cows. Sheep. Pigs. When I drop a jar of tomato paste which smashes on the floor, I think *grief brain*, and walk away. Grief brain is like baby brain but without the joy.

Neuroscience shows that trauma rewires the brain,

making it react to loss as it would to a predator. Faced with the monster of death, the limbic system, which controls the feelings and behaviours essential to survival, pushes the reasoning, decision-making prefrontal cortex aside, floods the body with the stress hormone cortisol and takes over the show. The centres of non-essential brain functions – the kind tasked with remembering the date, or whether you took your vitamin D, or where you left your mobile – are suppressed. Grief brain is what makes you lose the thread, or never find it in the first place. Grief brain is what triggers your rage at the careless presumption of an acquaintance who texts 'How are you?', assuming you owe them the pain and effort of replying to such a vast and monstrous question. Grief brain is what makes you ask the person you see in the mirror, but don't properly recognise: *Who are you? What are you? What exactly are you for?*

In the fruit aisle I pick up a pomegranate, one of the boys' favourite fruits as children. Demeter is the Greek goddess of the harvest and agriculture, presiding over grains and Earthly fertility. When her daughter Persephone is out picking flowers, the ground cracks open and Hades hauls her down to the underworld. It's by eating a few pomegranate seeds – the fruit that symbolises the indissolubility of marriage – that Persephone becomes trapped there. Demeter, mad with grief, hunts for her child everywhere, and prevents the earth from bearing fruit until she sees Persephone again. When she is finally allowed to meet her daughter, she secures a deal with Hades: for a few months of the year, Persephone can return to the world of light and live on earth again. I'd settle for a day, a minute, a second. I wouldn't even have to see my child: just knowing he was alive would be enough. But who do I strike that deal with, standing in a supermarket holding a pomegranate shipped in from Spain?

As I put it in my basket my phone rings. I'd forgotten my weekly counselling session session with Jenny, a volunteer from Cardiac Risk in the Young. Fifteen years ago, her son Nick died the same way as Raph: alive one minute, dead the next. When she asks me how I am I glance around, lower my voice and tell her straight out that I want to die.

'It's not that I'd kill myself. But if someone decided to push me under a bus, I'd be OK with it.'

'That's quite normal,' she says, unfazed. 'I felt that too.'

'And then you stopped?'

'I wanted it less. And then I stopped wanting it altogether.'

'How?'

'I spent four months painting walls. That helped.'

'Do you feel your son's still around?' I ask her.

Yes, she tells me. Once, when she was alone in her

garden, she was suddenly aware of the powerful, unmis-
takeable smell of his aftershave. My heart lifts in the same
way it lifted when one of Raph's activist friends told me
about the time her affinity group was planning a daring
protest action in his honour, and a fox showed up just
when they needed his courage the most.

'Do you have a good life?' I ask. I need to know this,
urgently.

'Yes,' she says, and she says it so fast and so unhesitatingly
that I know it's true. 'I would say I have a very good life.
A fulfilling life.'

'I'd like that to be me one day. But I don't know what
it would look like.'

'Nor did I. It comes with time, and work. It's the hardest
thing you'll ever have to do. Nobody can do it for you.
But you'll get there.'

Yes, I will, I think after we've hung up. *Because I want to.*

'And I want you to,' says Raph, biting into the pomegranate. He doesn't even peel it. And I feel my Covid
mask move, and I realise I'm smiling. The flash of sudden
pleasure makes me glad, but I no longer wish for happiness. Not because I have ruled it out, but because it has
come to feel superficial and egocentric to hold as a primary
goal. I want something deeper and more meaningful. When
I asked Jenny if she had a good life, she didn't say it was
happy: she said it was fulfilling. Fulfilment implies the

acknowledgement of other peoples' needs. It evokes the expanding organic tapestry of cross-relationships that thrives on symbiosis, encapsulated by the word *ubuntu*: 'I am because you are; you are because I am.' Aristotle knew this distinction, differentiating between *hedonia*, the transient happiness that comes from pleasure, and *eudaimonia*, the happiness that comes from living in a way that embodies meaning.

But fulfilment requires action. Every week I consider joining our weekly Writers Rebel Zoom meeting. And every week I fail to attend. I know that activism will deepen my roots in the wider world, and that the cause I share with Raphaël will renew and intensify my sense of purpose.

But I am not ready. First, the animal inside me must do its work. And I must trust it to.

One of my favourite photos that Raphaël took in Costa Rica is of his hand, with a sleek black viper, thin as a bootlace, coiled around his wrist. He'd been about to put his camera away when he felt a movement on his left forearm. And there it was, coiled around his watch and home-made bracelets. It's pinned to our fridge, across from the kitchen table where we're sitting, and, while he plays with the snake, I'm reminiscing about his eccentric use of cutlery. When he was little, he copied everything his brother did. And since Matti is left-handed, Raphaël trained himself to eat with the knife in his left hand and the fork in the right.

'Then Matti switched his cutlery round too, remember? And you both kept it up. So I now have a left-handed adult son who holds the fork in his right hand and a right-handed adult son who holds the fork in his left. You both trained yourselves to do something against your nature.'

He smiles. Both boys, so similar and yet so different. Raphaël calls me Mama or *Madre*, and Matti calls me Ma.

'But you both say Mother when I annoy you.'

'Wrong tense. I'm dead, remember? You keep doing that.'

'What am I supposed to say? Do you really want me to change my verb tenses just because you died?'

'Hey. The bereaved make the rules,' he says, watching the viper coil around his wrist.

'How come I thought about you so much the month before you died?' I ask him. 'Why were you on my mind far more than usual? How come we spoke so often, in that month? I should have stopped you going on that trip.'

He smiles, but there's sadness in it. 'Nothing could have stopped me going. You know that. Everybody knew it.'

We sit in silence, while the snake laces itself through his fingers.

'Are you homesick, Raph?'

'I don't need to be. I'm here.'

'So what's it like, being dead?'

But I get no answer. He and his little black viper have gone.

Am I mad, conjuring my dead child like this? Am I mad, to be worrying already about how to celebrate his next birthday, the first one he won't be alive for, and wondering how to get through the first anniversary of his death without crying all day? Am I mad to have become convinced that the day of his death marked the beginning of a new, surreal reverse pregnancy that will culminate in his vanishing altogether from my cells to a place before conception: the before-life state that is also the afterlife state or perhaps simply pure consciousness, or pure nothingness? How do our relationships with the disembodied live on, except through belief, force of will, yearning, magical thinking, imagination and metaphor?

I don't know. But I mark November 6th in my calendar.

On a grief podcast, I hear about a bereaved father who can immediately identify other parents who have lost a child, because 'you can smell the smoke on them'. If that father walked into my kitchen now, would he smell the smoke on me and my friend Charlotte, as we sit at the table eating marinaded herring? Outside, the faint spring sun comes and goes, and children's voices drift up from the courtyard below. Five years ago, Charlotte's youngest son Frederik, barely in his twenties, took his own life.

Recently my reverse pregnancy has been feeling more of a physical reality than a metaphor, and as the days pass my body seems to bloat with the growing emptiness inside me. *The absence of presence and the presence of absence*: when I come across this phrase, it sums up the vastness of my inner vacuum. Charlotte shows no surprise when I tell her about the metaphor I have conjured. She experienced something similar, she tells me. Not long before Frederik's funeral she was drinking coffee with the priest.

'And suddenly, out of the blue, I felt this long, painful contraction, deep inside my uterus. The muscles were tightening up with a force I didn't know it could still have. And it went on. Somehow, I'd gone into a kind of labour.'

'What did you do?'

'I breathed in and out with each contraction, like you do in childbirth. Deep breath in, slow breath out.'

'Did you tell the priest what was going on?'

'Yes. I had to. He could see something was happening. But he took it very calmly. He said, "It's OK. You're giving birth to a new Frederik."'

'And were you?'

'Yes. In a way,' she says. 'It makes sense. Frederik lived in my body for nine months. And my body knew that the life it once contained had stopped. And so it went into labour. It knew exactly what it was doing.'

After she leaves I think: I don't just want a new Raphaël to be born. I want a new *me* to be born. I want his death to reveal something fresh, and urgent, and alive, and above all meaningful. There is a Japanese proverb that runs *fall down seven times, get up eight*. Is this how to reach the future version of myself who is older and wiser than me, and has some answers? To fall again, and again, and again, and to stubbornly get up every time? And keep on walking? If it weren't possible, the streets would be littered with the bodies of those who said, 'I can't go on.' And meant it. ('I couldn't cope at all if it happened to me,' people sometimes say to me, as if I have *chosen to cope*. For the record, I haven't, and I'm not.) Yes, I want a future version of me to discover the universe all over again: to be stronger and more capacious, to feel more, know more, understand more, to love more and love better, to be kind, to do what's in my power to make things right instead of wrong. When I was pregnant, I ate for two. Now I am living for two. And I want to make the time that's left to us matter.

After that day, by tiny increments, I become more active. The Baltic is cold, but I begin to take occasional swims in the nearby harbour. With the jellyfish pulsing alongside me beneath the glassy surface, I can forget everything except the present moment: its taste, its smell, its texture, and the sounds that reverberate through it. This strengthens me. It seems that, in the timeless parenthesis of grief and lockdown, I'm not alone in discovering that less is more, and that every still moment contains – if you look for it – an opportunity to feel freshly and radically present in the world.

Raphaël knew this. Beneath a photo of two girls who came to his nature retreat last summer in France, he writes of their intuitive connection to one another, and to the natural world. 'It seemed everything they did was an embodied exercise in tantric, mindful play. They enjoyed every moment, every minute, every bite of food. I was jealously mesmerised. To survive climate breakdown and ecological collapse, humanity desperately needs a restructuring of consciousness to redefine our relationship with the natural world. It warms my heart to see people well on their way through that paradigm shift, redefining what it means to be human.' He'd told me about these visitors: how they'd encouraged him to slow down, take off his wristwatch and just be in the moment. How it opened his eyes. Many of his friends told me that in his last year he was learning to be less driven, and to tend his body and his soul. He'd meditated for years, but now he started doing yoga. He was becoming more open to nuance, and trying to slow down and enjoy the subtle resonances of all around him. Moment by moment, he was deepening.

And now, through him, I am trying to learn, as he did, to pay proper heed to the quiet flashes of pleasure that every day brings, even the very worst ones when I can barely function: the way the neck plumage of my pink-brown pigeon shimmers and pearls in the light; the heady, butterscotch smell of the buds on our little indoor orange tree; the earthy taste of nuts roasted with spices; the boom of the cannon, symbolically fired at dawn and dusk at the old garrison near the harbour. When delight bloomed for Kurt Vonnegut, he would always say: 'Well if this isn't nice, I don't know what is.' Whenever I find a moment of joy, I decide, however fleeting, I'll mark it in Raphaël's honour and make it his as well as mine. In that way, the next version of myself will appreciate every tiny epiphany more and give it the reverence it's due. Perhaps, in this hurtling age, every such moment will come to feel more intense, more freighted with significance and more worthy of gratitude. Maybe then, the truth that we are part of the huge, intricate web of life will reclaim its rightful place. But for now, if the rucksack of stones on my back feels lighter or I even forget it's there, or if I have a physical sensation of wellbeing, I say so. Aloud.

Sometimes, the woman whose son died does not feel broken every second of every day. Sometimes, the woman whose son died feels good. Sometimes, just a couple of months after his death, she smiles and laughs.

CHAPTER 10: WILL YOU REACH TIPPING POINTS?

The sun is shining on the red rooftops of the city, and the wisteria is snaking new tendrils through the balcony rails. But today, as I put out grain for the pigeons and mutter aloud to myself, I'm not smiling or laughing. Today, I'm stubbornly resistant to enchantment.

'The neighbours downstairs are complaining about the birdshit,' I tell Raphaël. 'They sent me a text. The pigeons are shitting over the rail. It lands on their plants.' He laughs. 'Chill. Just move the birdfeeder over there, so the shit lands on our balcony instead.' I move it. 'See? And you get a better view from the kitchen window. Bingo.' He stops. 'Wow. You're still angry.'

'Of course I'm fucking angry. They have four kids living

at home. I have two children. One lives in another country and the other one's dead.' He quirks his magnificent, pierced eyebrow, and the tiny golden stud shoots out light. 'And did you hear the news just now?' I won't let go of my rage. 'Just this month: lethal floods in Rwanda, Brazil, Pakistan and Tanzania. Locust swarms in Kenya. Bushfires in China. Tens of thousands of almond trees felled by a storm in Turkey. Carbon emissions are down but they'll go right up again when the pandemic's over because people – *people I know* – just want things to go back to normal and start taking weekend city break again. History will look back on this moment and say what the fuck. But for now people like us are treated like freaks for thinking there's a bigger threat than a pandemic. No one wants to know, and no one's going to learn from this.'

He flicks his long braid against his hand. 'Some people are. You'll see. Lighten up, Mama.'

'I can't. You're dead.'

He smiles. 'Define dead.'

I can't.

I can't define grief either, but I know it is radicalising me. I am already becoming more certain about who and what I need to surround myself with; how I should and shouldn't spend the years that are left to me; what matters and what doesn't. But grief also makes everything seem

YOUR WILD AND PRECIOUS LIFE

more fragile. Just as the faulty electrical signals of Raph's heart had a tipping point, so I'm aware of other tipping points, and how kairos manifests: a long gestation, followed by a point past which it's all too late. The pandemic didn't come from nowhere, any more than the wider era of ecological and civilisational upheaval we were all born into did. Kairos events, which can unfold over seconds, minutes, hours, days, months, years and centuries, can take many forms: sudden geological upheavals, slower environmental shifts, alterations in collective mental pressure and accretions of belief and thought that spark wars, mass movements, enlightenments and revolutions. The human population has doubled since I was born, and in each decade of my life our species has pumped more carbon into the atmosphere than ever before. When you know something, you can't un-know it. I can't pretend that Raphaël isn't dead, or that wildlife is as abundant and unthreatened as in my childhood, or that one million wildlife species aren't hurtling towards extinction, or that the planet isn't choking as it cooks. And the short-sightedness. Faced with clear evidence, you can fool your own brain for a while, but not for ever. But still I'm tempted to do nothing, because how can I move open-eyed into a future that feels so daunting, given the time that's left to do what's needed?

I once met a climatologist who spent much of her

time studying snow and ice. Like many of her colleagues, she had found and measured evidence of the Earth's warming for herself. Seeing where it took her thoughts, she told me she sometimes wished she knew less. Yet she incarnated a very human paradox. To many people who understand the stakes, the question of whether to bring another human life into the world can feel existential. After some soul-searching, she decided to have a baby, despite knowing that long before her son reaches the age of a hundred that futurologists blithely forecast for him, he is very likely to inhabit a world inconceivably different from our own. Sea-level rise will have submerged entire islands and re-drawn coastlines. The droughts, wildfires, storms, heat-domes and crop failures that lead to sickness, starvation and wars today will have intensified exponentially, rendering much of the world uninhabitable. And nothing will feel permanent. When I asked her how she decided to risk having a child, she went silent for a moment. Biology is the short, easy answer, she said eventually. But you can over-ride biology, and some choose to. The longer, trickier truth is cognitive dissonance.

F. Scott Fitzgerald said: 'The test of a first-rate intelligence is the ability to carry two opposed ideas in mind at the same time and still retain the ability to function.' I knew the climatologist to have first-rate intelligence. And she used it, daily, to divide herself in two. One version of her, the scientist, had its eyes wide open and it grieved. The other, the mother, was blind. And with a great, deep force, it loved. It protected. And it trusted. Raphaël did the same. His Instagram feed is full of images and commentaries about snakes, insects, birds, tigers, bats, monkeys, turtles and coral reefs. I'm drawn to one image in particular: not of a creature, but of a constellation of rich green diamond leaves floating on a pool of night-dark water. He rarely took plant images, but I can see why this one spoke to him. Humans evolved to recognise and love the branching, repeating patterns of such fractal growth: the outward and onward spreading of organic forms of every shape and size, nested in the wider structures of a deeper life-force.

'The small is not insignificant', he writes. 'Each living creature, no matter its size, has been carved to the peak of survival efficiency by millennia of natural selection. Look into the patterns of biology and find history.' I urge those patterns to endure even in the midst of their visible annihilation. This year saw the Earth's hottest January since records began; the number of animals killed or displaced by the Australian bush fires is creeping towards three billion; and the extent of sea ice in Antarctica was at an all-time minimum for February – for the second consecutive year. In that context, to extrapolate is to acknowledge that much of the planet is on track to become uninhabitable in the lifetime of any baby born today. And yet I keep trusting, as the climatologist trusts, and as Raphaël trusted, that the patterns of biology will find a way to endure and evolve.

And if those patterns can endure and evolve, why not other patterns? The shock of Raphael's death reverberates within the wider shock of the pandemic – which in turn is part of the rolling shock of climate and ecological breakdown of which it is a symptom. All three kairos events, nested like matryoshka dolls, require specific survival mechanisms – but there are also parallels in the emotional reactions that they trigger, which could hold the key to a new way of being. It was the climate scientist and Nobel laureate Steve W. Running who first likened the phases of ecological grief to those described by the psychologist Elisabeth Kübler-Ross in her work with the dying. Kübler-Ross would turn in her grave if she knew to what extent her famous Five Phases of Grief had been misinterpreted as a blueprint for a 'classic' grieving process, but the characteristics she noted remain helpful and can be applied by extension to wider emergencies.

First there's denial – characterised by the belief that the crisis isn't happening, or that humans aren't the root cause. Next comes the anger phase, when you realise your self-image, world view or lifestyle will have to change substantially. Then comes bargaining, which can take the form of thinking, wishfully, that the situation may have been exaggerated, and that any problem that science can identify, it can also solve. Depression comes when you feel overwhelmed by the scale of what is happening, and realise that governments and corporations are not only spinning their wheels but often actively exacerbating the damage. The final stage is acceptance – like assimilating the truth that you will never see your loved one again, or that viruses can jump species and mutate in frightening ways and may do so again, or recognising that it's impossible to refute the scientific evidence of the escalating climate crisis – and looking for solutions. Steve Running admits there's no evidence to show that global warming can be stopped in its tracks – but concludes that 'doing nothing is unconscionable'. Raphaël refused to do nothing, and so must I. Like him, and like the climatologist, I must keep trusting – and I must act. But how does action work, when I'm so broken I can barely function?

The Japanese art of *kintsugi* – the repair of fractured porcelain with *urushi*, a lacquer mixed with gold dust – emphasises fragility with a colour symbolising worth. After the amputation of Raph's death, I need to summon the elemental force that insists on life and its continuation. Whatever scar tissue grows over my wound, I know I'll never feel or be the same again.

But I will still exist, and persist. And perhaps one day

I will live fully again, but in a different way. 'Hope is not the conviction that something will turn out well,' wrote Václav Havel, 'but the certainty that something is worth doing no matter how it turns out.' So now, when I lose hope that the life-force that I need is still inside me, my hope is as simple as Raphaël's for the planet. I hope for a return of active hope: of the will that finds the way. Not just for me, but for the world.

CHAPTER II: WILL YOUR ELEPHANTS COME?

He's been captured in a jungle and he's condemned to death. We're scrambling to get there before they kill him, but it's too late: suddenly a video feed shows us that Raphaël's alone, and he has a gun. Without speaking, he conveys that to avoid execution he's going to shoot himself. I shriek *tell them to kill me instead!* There's a silent bang and I burst awake with the dream clinging to me like filth.

It's a bargaining dream, but when I remember his last Instagram post – two fingers pointed at his head like a gun, captioned with the question 'Would you risk your life to defend wildlife?' – I wonder if it's telling me something else too. Wildlife workers and indigenous Earth protectors are murdered with terrifying frequency. In the defence speech Raphaël prepared in court for a trial he would never live to see, he wrote about the indigenous tribes in Amazonia in whose name he and his fellow-activists vandalised the Brazilian Embassy in London: 'They know exactly what happens when men with guns enter their lands in search of money. It's been happening to them for over 500 years, since South America was first colonised. Genocide. Isolated tribes contacted without their consent, and then wiped out. Hundreds, thousands, millions dead from diseases which they have no immunity to.'

Raphaël intended to go back to the Amazon. Was the purpose of the nightmare to give me an idea of another, worse scenario? If that's the case, it's done its work, and I feel a surge of gratitude that he died the way he did. That he was running, and singing, and urging others on when he fell. That he was in his element and doing what he loved.

I hold this thought close to me when I grieve for the future he will never have, the man he would have become, the children he might one day have fathered.

I go to visit Thomas, who first introduced me to the Terrible Club. His garden path is fringed with delicate pink roses, which smell intense and otherworldly in the bright spring sun. Hungry to learn how he navigates the future without his daughter, I join him in his dining-room overlooking the lawn and we talk about losing our children and getting stuck. About how sometimes emerging is about taking a simple decision: to take a walk, to do something new, to cook a meal.

'When she was alive, Ida lit up this home,' says Thomas.

'Do you talk to her?'

Yes. He does.

He shows me a picture. Ida is youth itself: beautiful, radiant youth. She died a year ago. He was directing a film at the time, and within weeks of her death he went back to work. He knew from his silent conversations with her that she'd be urging him on.

'The film became a kind of monument to her,' he says. 'She knew all the cast and crew and she inspired the manuscript. We made it in her name.'

We talk about how we can continue to honour our children and keep them alive through what we do and convey as we search for a sense of meaning in what has happened. I tell him that I have been writing about Raphaël as a form of therapy, but perhaps one day some of what I write might make sense to other people who are grieving, in whatever way. I tell him that when I'm in doubt about something, I ask Raphaël, and he gives me the answer. Thomas starts to cry, and suddenly I'm crying too. As we sit at his table, weeping quietly for for

Raph and Ida, I feel our separate pains merge into the vast pain of all devastating losses: a great, shared wounding that contains the seed of something that might one day transform us, if we can find a way to let it. Back home, my crying is harder than ever, as if I could vomit out my pain.

'I was there, Mama,' Raphaël says, as I wipe away my tears. 'In the roses. With Ida. She's there a lot. In that house and in the garden.'

I hear him say this because I'm clairaudient.

I hear him say this because I have conjured it.

I hear him say this because his foetal cells are still inside me.

I hear him say this because I am deranged.

I hear him say this because he was there.

You choose.

When an elephant mother loses her child, the other elephants circle around her to help her through her grief. I already knew Thomas and several other members of the Terrible Club before Raphaël died, and now that I'm a member too, I'm getting to know more. It's the worst club in the world, but it contains fellowship, enormous kindness, and the level of empathy that no-one outside the club can offer, however sincere and heartfelt their intentions. Other friends and acquaintances text, instructing me to *Call me any time if you'd like to talk*. But although they mean well, they don't know what they're asking of me; don't realise that I don't have the energy to make phone calls; that so much is beyond me now; that I am past etiquette. The people I communicate with most apart from Carsten and my closest family are those who force an agenda on me. Friends who say: *I'm taking you out for a walk at 11 o'clock on Wednesday,* or *I'm coming with food at 6,* or *I'm calling you at 12: pick up if you can but I won't be offended if you don't.* These, too, are my elephants.

But someone vital – someone I thought would be among my elephants – has vanished from my life.

'Just let her go,' says Matti when I tell him. 'You don't need friends like that.'

He's right, but after a month of silence I find myself sending her a text saying that I miss her, and although I know death scares her I'm still confused that she hasn't been in touch. I end it: 'I say this with love'.

Two long days pass before she replies. Her message is worded carefully, and unequivocally. She is sorry I might have found her cold and distant but she's struggled to find the right language to console me. She's falling short of my expectations, but 'perhaps those expectations are too exacting'.

I'm too crushed to answer, and anyway, what's the point in begging someone for something they've announced they cannot and will not give? My rational mind insists on this, but grief isn't rational, and as the weeks pass, my sense of betrayal curdles into demonic rage, a rage that isn't just about her, but about the amount of energy I'm using to tend a fresh wound I never asked for. Why am I wasting so much emotional energy on the one friend who let me down, when all the others didn't, and why can't I stop? Fury saps my spirit, intensifying my pain and adding poison to the mix.

Until she resigned as my friend, I hadn't known that it's commonplace in the West for grievers to suffer brutal rejections from friends and acquaintances. But now the monstrous fact must sit in me and settle. Many cultures have elaborate rituals and conventions around death, just as Britain once did: as recently as the Victorian era, when death was common, people wore black armbands to signal their bereavement. Now, modern medicine gives us the questionable luxury of sanitising and compartmentalising death so effectively that instead of being seen as a natural transition, it's a 'failed outcome'. So we ghost grief, avoiding the newly bereaved as if they are bearers of contamination, and paring down our rituals as if to foreclose our pain.

But, paradoxically, when I turn on any screen, death is everywhere. Killing after killing, crime scene after crime scene, corpse after corpse, morgue after morgue, funeral after funeral. In another life, the life before this, I was often voyeuristically beguiled by such scenes, perhaps almost pruriently hungry for them. But now they fill me with such revulsion that I recoil and turn away, traumatised all over again. How did I ever see this as 'entertainment'? In crime fiction, it's as if death itself is the crime, and its solving is our redemption. Such thrillers – including books I myself have written – don't encourage us to speculate about the existence of a greater consciousness, but about the identity of the criminal. It makes me wonder if the modern world's appetite for screen depictions of death is the modern equivalent of rote prayer: a personal and societal calming mechanism that reassures us that every detective's case file contains an answer, backed by forensic evidence, to what is fundamentally an existential question. And while the body count on any given Netflix evening could be in the hundreds or even thousands, how often have you seen a plausible depiction of grief on screen? And how can people express compassion for the grieving if there are so few templates for expressing it beyond a Hallmark sympathy card?

If I ran a school, here's what I'd teach the kids to say to the parent or friend or sibling of a dead child. I'd teach them that in the face of something they can't imagine, it's better to say something, however inadequate it may feel, than to say nothing. I'd teach them that saying nothing is to rub salt into an open wound. I'd teach them that staying silent in the face of an uncomfortable truth – be it death or climate breakdown or mass extinction – is more than active cowardice. It's passive violence.

Amidst all my questioning and raging and my daily struggle to consider my life worth living, Raphaël is everywhere: the permanent, invisible elephant I talk to every day, and whose answers to my questions – whether conjured from memory, imagination, intuition, language, or pure longing – smooth the jagged edges of my pain. But his death is another kind of elephant. It's the elephant that fills every room I enter. It needs special handling. If I speak its name and tend to it, something new might grow in me. And perhaps through my own expansion, a time will come when I match the elephant in scale, and another time when I outgrow it, so it no longer eclipses me, but stands in my shadow.

Writing offers a different kind of solace. When E.M. Forster asked 'How can I know what I think until I see what I say?', he encapsulated the way thought is alchemised by language. Writing has always been my most accessible form of therapy, but never more so than now. To write is to explore beyond the outer edges of the map until a truth appears that sends a depth-charge though the blood; to interrogate the dance of light and dark on the cave wall as the fire of the psyche flickers; to ride the rapids of a thought experiment as far as it will go, and further. Most of what I write feels like the desperate whimpering of an animal caught in a trap. But increasingly, in the margins, I catch other notes that hint at a quest that's part self-interrogation about how to live, part pantheistic prayer, part evidence that something new is germinating inside me. I get the sense that a new dimension is opening to me, and that I'm part of a vast network of understandings reached by others who have lost children and found ways to assimilate and grow around their grief, as an oyster grows a pearl around a painfully chafing grain of sand: slowly, by instinct, habit and accretion. Everything I am feeling, countless others have felt before me and feel with me, and will come to feel. There's a bittersweet sense of validation in knowing there's a silent army of grieving parents walking the same path I'm treading now, and that they've been there all along. I had thought it a lonely path, but I'm realising it's the opposite. And alongside us, at the periphery of our vision, walk those we have lost. It is as if, like Rilke's notion of God, we are 'webbing made / Of a hundred roots, that drink in silence'; microscopic elements of a vast subterranean organism connected to other living beings in a matrix as complex and rich as the mycelium web beneath the forest floor. Part of a whispered conversation that reflects a timeless process of renewal and decay.

CHAPTER 12: WILL THE BIRDS BRING MESSAGES?

We measure a baby's age from the moment of birth: first in minutes and hours, then days, then weeks, then months, then years. As new parents, we use these markers because the changes we see are as endlessly astonishing as babies themselves: little time-travellers who have never heard of time, freshly arrived from a dimension whose existence – either as pure nothing or as pure everything – cannot be measured or proved, any more than consciousness itself can. Raphaël was a minute old, then an hour old, then a day, a week, a month, a year, then a boy, a teenager and a young man. And then he was twenty-five years, four months and six days old. And then he was dead.

Tomorrow, just as he was once three months old, he will be three months dead.

'I need a sign tomorrow, Raph,' I tell him. 'I mean it.'

'He was the brightest of all of us on the zoology course,' says his friend Henry, when we speak the next day on the phone. 'But he could be a real tit.'

I laugh. 'What kind of a tit?'

'On social occasions, he could just really put his foot in it. There'd be situations when we were all thinking the same thing, but not saying it because it wasn't appropriate. But Iggy would just come right out with it.'

Afterwards, when I recount this to Carsten, I have to explain the word 'tit'.

'Like a breast?'

'Same word, but it means an idiot in the same way dick does.'

That afternoon, the word tit is on my mind. How did dick and tit become synonymous with idiot, while prick and cunt are cruder and more vicious? And why do things go 'tits up'?

I wander into the kitchen, where the double doors to the balcony stand open, then I laugh aloud.

Settled on top of the left-hand door is a tiny, fragile bird with a greenish-yellow breast, angular wing-blades, and a black helmet and bib. I have long complained that we never see small birds on our balcony, and that pigeons – though I love them – are our only visitors. But this bird is unmistakably a great tit. What's more, it's almost inside the kitchen – as if at any moment it might just flutter in.

'Raph!' My shriek of excitement scares it off, and brings Carsten in, alarmed.

'Raph was here,' I tell him, elated. 'There was one tit I forgot about. A great tit. A *musvit*. He came and made a joke.'

A bird theme is emerging in Raphaël's visits. First the dancing red-tailed bird, my daily visits from the pink-brown pigeon, and now – the day after I asked for a sign – the *musvit*. It's as if Raphaël knows what I need, and he's doing what he can. Many cultures believe that birds are spiritual beings, capable of acting as messengers between the living and the dead. Perhaps they are right to. For the next few days, I feel a lightness round me. Then doubt creeps in.

In *The Other Side of Sadness*, George A. Bonanno observes how bereaved people tortured by grief imagine signs of communication from a lost loved one. Often, it comes in the form of an animal. But whatever comfort the signs bring, he says, it never seems to last. 'Initially, perhaps, there is a kind of anticipation, almost excitement, but then comes the sobering up: The new relationship is limited. It could be no other way.' Will there come a time when I, too, 'sober up'? Will the red-tailed bird in South Africa and the pink-brown pigeon on my balcony and the *musvit* come to seem like ridiculous, banal symbols not of Raphaël's continued presence, but my desperation? Or is something else at work?

Carl Jung, who became fascinated with the paranormal, coined the term synchronicity to describe a 'meaningful coincidence of two or more events where something other than the probability of chance is involved'. He believed that synchronicities have an illuminative if unprovable purpose, and that convergent events embody a phenomenon that taps our inner potential, enabling us to constellate our individual consciousness within a greater whole. I can choose between two options: to trust my rational mind, or trust my instinct – which tells me that my premonition that I would lose a child, Raphaël's heightened awareness of his own mortality, the red-tailed bird in South Africa, the pigeon I commune with every morning, and the *musvit* perched on the balcony door are significant. And so what if I can't prove they are? I have never believed in what others call God, but since Raphaël's death, I'm no longer able to dismiss the possibility that we are part of an omniscient and omnipresent consciousness. Ralph Waldo Emerson, who led the transcendentalist movement of the mid-nineteenth century, coined the term 'oversoul' to describe a being that pervades the universe and encompasses all human and non-human souls. His intimation of the intrinsic enmeshment of living things strikes a chord in me. Not only because it plays out in every individual ecosystem and in the planetary ecosystem of which each is a part, but because it underscores my doubt that the mechanistic mindset of the culture I grew up in has served me well. As a result of this mindset most people in the West – publicly, at least – are quick to belittle or dismiss the idea of communication with other dimensions, even though string theory posits that the universe operates within ten dimensions which include the familiar ones of length, width, depth and time. The more I consider this paradox, the more absurd it seems that it's socially acceptable to declare faith in an ancient patriarchal god, but socially unsettling to say you sense the presence of the dead.

To hell with social acceptability. Clouds of glory trailed behind us when we were born, as they trail behind everyone in deep contact with the Wild. Every day on shores, in fields and forests and wedges of city green, young human animals become one with the pink writhing of an earthworm, the dance of sunlight through apple leaves, the smell of fungi, the texture of bark, the blackbird's song. I remember feeling this porousness as a young child: this deep trust that whatever I felt was somehow echoed back. Intuition is a form of perception: a muscle that we under-use or outright disrespect. In not embracing it enough in my adulthood, I've narrowed rather than expanded my mind. It's a big realisation to dawn at the age of sixty. But with it comes the understanding that what can't be labelled as a fact doesn't warrant instant dismissal.

The strongest evidence of this – and a point of inter-section between science and spirituality – is the phenomenon known as the Near–Death Experience, or the NDE. People have reported coming back from the dead for centuries, but with the advances in medicine in the last century, many thousands of people have technically died and then come back to life, often after being pronounced dead. Many of them report remembering experiences which changed them profoundly. Typically, they enter a space filled with light, love and a sense of universal connectedness incomparable to anything they felt before. And when they return to life – sometimes accurately reporting operating-room details and medical conversations they could not possibly have known about when technically dead – they no longer fear death and are instilled with a profound sense of meaning that calls on them to change the way they live.

I think of Raph's bucket list. He ticked off a lot. He touched many tigers and survived. Performing terrifying cliff-dives, he flew without wings.

'And you got that NDE you wanted.'

'I did.'

'But it was really just a DE. Because you didn't come back.'

He smiles. 'Come on. I never left.'

Pinecones crunch beneath our feet amid the leaf-litter that has survived the winter and, in the distance, there's the buzz of a wood-saw. But beyond that, it's strangely quiet. We're on a rare outing from the locked-down city, walking on sandy pathways among the beech and birch and fir. Denmark, the most intensively farmed nation in Europe, has eradicated a vast swathe of birds and, in Raphaël's lifetime, exterminated 95 per cent of its insect life. We are walking among ghosts. So when a lone yellow butterfly flits amid the pale greys, greens and browns of the woodland, I fixate on it and follow its zig-zag flight from shrub to flower to tree. It stops only briefly in each place, and I try to fathom what it wants; to work out if there is some kind of pattern to its route; how it chooses which flower to alight on; to detect some method in its insect madness.

It's no surprise that, like birds, butterflies are totemic creatures for the grieving, or of those who would console them. It's hard to resist seeing them as winged messengers, or to refuse the metaphors of metamorphosis and transcendence that they offer. In ancient Greece, the butterfly symbolised the human soul. As short-lived icons of grace and beauty, they adorn condolence cards and headstones in a way no other insect could, with the possible exception of the scarab beetle, which symbolised rebirth and regeneration to the ancient Egyptians.

I sit on a fallen tree-trunk and stare into space, stuck between worlds.

'In the bardo again?' whispers Raph.

'Where else? It's where I live.'

'You're just growing. And growing hurts, OK?'

'You died so young.'

'I died when I was supposed to.'

'Am I meant to find solace in the fact that your heart was a time bomb? Well I don't.'

'Try being glad I was alive as long as I was, instead of raging that I died so young.'

'But you didn't get a full lifetime.'

'Yes I did,' he says quietly. 'My lifetime was full.'

'How could it be full, when you died at twenty-five?'

He smiles. 'It was full of my life.'

On the way home, Carsten and I drift into a bookshop and browse the tables. We're the only customers. The bookseller – a man my age or a little younger – hovers near me, then asks me if I'm looking for anything in particular.

'Do you have any books about grief?'

His face changes, and he hurries me to the far end of the bookshop where the self-help and spirituality books are kept.

'This one helped me a lot,' he says, pointing to one. 'And this one.' He indicates another.

The air around us stills. 'May I ask you who you lost?' I ask.

His eyes well up. 'My daughter. Cot death. Thirty years ago.'

So he, too, is a member of the Terrible Club. I tell him about Raph's painfully recent death.

'Does it get any easier?' I ask.

It does, he says. 'But there are still some days when . . .' He makes a hopeless gesture. He and his wife still celebrate her birthday, he says. 'We can't forget her and we don't want to.'

'Do you feel she's still around?' It's the first time I've asked this of a stranger.

He smiles through his tears. 'Yes. I feel her now.'

'How?'

'You came into my shop. She sent you.'

Back home, as I think about the silent woods we walked in, and the insect ghosts that seemed to haunt them, and the bookseller's baby daughter, and how a caterpillar becomes a butterfly without ever knowing how, it comes to me that a being retains its essence by transmuting into whatever state comes next, be it a new physical form or a memory or a vibrant, active presence in a dimension that is just a blink away.

And that if I stay open to this thought, it can take me forward into the next phase, and all that it brings.

PART THREE: SUMMER

CHAPTER 13: WILL YOU BE A DROP IN THE OCEAN?

In the heart of London, three young bodies lie curled on a gallery floor in the foetal position, their naked skin slicked with glistening black oil. It could be an artwork by an AI tasked with creating a contemporary mash-up of Goya and Rembrandt – but it's an action by the XR Snowflakes Affinity Group: the semi-naked bodies are those of activists, and the oil is fake. It's the autumn of 2019, and the group is demonstrating at the National Portrait Gallery in London, where the fossil fuel behemoth BP is sponsoring its annual portrait competition. After covering a space on the floor, the three activists have stripped off and positioned themselves on it, and Raphaël has whipped out the bottle of black liquid and poured it over them, while a fifth activist takes photographs. It's the work of a few minutes, and when they're done, they slip out again, unnoticed.

I remember Raphaël's pride afterwards at the media splash it made. He never lived to learn that the National Portrait Gallery would go on to announce that it would be cutting its ties with BP after thirty years.

'So is this a win, a drop in the ocean, or both?' I ask him.

He smiles. 'Don't underestimate drops of water. What are tsunamis and avalanches made of? It's the same with mass movements. Every drop matters.'

'I still have your number in my phone, under Favourites. I can't delete it. And I can't call it, either.'

He cocks an eyebrow. 'You could.'

'I don't dare. You might not answer.'

He flashes me a smile. 'Perhaps one day I'll ring.'

'Did it feel beautiful, to be dying?'

'Of course it did. It was fucking awesome.' Is he telling me the truth, or just what I need to hear?

Danish summer can be capricious, but there is one constant: at its height, daylight arrives at 3 a.m. and stays till 11 p.m. June brings a new wave of sleeplessness. No longer able to push his death to a corner of my mind for an hour, or even a minute, I wake at four most days, suffused with a dread so unbearable that it catapults me out of bed. There's no logic to my fear. The worst has already happened. But the Dread is there and my only counter-measure is to shift to another location in a vain attempt to remove myself from the equation. C.S. Lewis had the same physical sensation when he was grieving, noting: 'No one ever told me that grief was so much like fear. I am not afraid, but the sensation is like being afraid.' The rest-lessness I felt in South Africa has come back with force. Again, I want to be anywhere but in my own skin. The world is full of light but I'm being pulled backwards by the dark, urgent, futile craving for what I can't have. What does craving transform into? Where does that vicious, stubborn energy go? Epictetus, the freed slave who taught Stoic philosophy in ancient Greece and Rome, wrote: 'You too should remind yourself that what you love is mortal, that what you love is not your own . . . So if you long for your son or your friend when he is not granted to you, know that you are longing for a fig in winter.'

My longing is for a fig in winter. I'm not the only one missing him. Raph's partner Kira was one of the first people in his closest circle to contact me after he died, and one of several I am in touch with, tentatively and sporadically. The pain of talking about him is always biting but our first conversation since Raphaël's memorial in

London is easy and immediate. Like his other beloved partner, Savannah, Kira shares my conviction that Raphaël is still around – and my sense of always knowing what he'd say if he were here.

'You know the last thing he said to me?' she says. 'He called me from Johannesburg. And when we said goodbye he said, "OK, I'm off to play with the unicorns."'

Smiling at this, I drive out of Copenhagen to meet a new friend who reached out to me because she, too, has lost a child. Pia is elegant and kind. A yoga teacher, she bears her body with grace as she leads me into a sun-drenched garden filled with hollyhocks and arrow-head irises, and gestures to a table where we sit. Pia is three years into her grief for her son, and I four months, so the smoke on me is thicker. But as we talk, I smell it on her too. Over home-made bread and rhubarb compote, our conversation is by turns tear-streaked, reflective, raw, tender, brutal – and exhausting. If grief is love without a home, then despite the loveliness of the garden, we both feel homeless without our sons. We speak carefully, aware of triggering more pain. Or in a rush. We occasionally pause at length between blurted revelations, watching the flowers shift in the summer breeze, and sigh. Defeat, and longing. Figs in winter.

'Do you sense Raph's still with you?' Pia asks me. The question is tentative, but my answer isn't. I need to share this.

'Yes. He's with me a lot. We talk every day.'

She nods. 'Me and Noa too.'

In that moment of recognition our relationship shifts to a new gear. In an urgent rush, we talk about how we feel their presence, and the notion that energy doesn't disappear, but just transforms. Like me, Pia is pulled between an attachment to science and a deeper instinct that there is another dimension alongside ours, on a frequency that reaches us if we're open to it. She shows me the books she collected after Noa's death, and we exchange recommendations. Neither of us would have countenanced visiting the Spirituality section of a book-shop before we lost our sons, let alone the niche sub-section called Afterlife. We commiserate about the fact that we're now drawn there but we recoil from the jacket designs, with their pale yellow, white and mauve evocations of celestial light-sources and penchant for angel and cloud motifs. We feel queasy about the genre's vocabulary, too: 'beyond the veil', 'passing on', 'transitioning', 'on the other side', 'graduating from Earth-school', 'Angelversaries' and 'Heaven'.

'But after a while you get used to it,' says Pia, stoically. 'And what other language is there?'

She's right. This is the Wild West. She and I have gone through emotional near-death experiences of our own, and emerged – like NDE 'returners' – with the sense that another realm of consciousness exists, and that our intuition of it is something we must honour and explore. Part of Pia's transformation, she tells me, was due to a breakthrough encounter with a celebrated American medium who channels the spirits of the dead with notable accuracy. I have already heard of Suzanne Giesemann. Her background as a former US navy commander who was aide to the Chairman of the Joint Chiefs of Staff seems an unlikely one for a medium, but perhaps it's exactly that contrast that gives her heft. Quantum physics and neuroscience go some way towards explaining why under electrophysiological tests, experienced mediums and meditators have been shown to access gamma brain waves when in the transcendent state – an ability that enables Giesemann and others to access what has been called the 'afterlife frequency'.

'I never share what went on in that reading outside the family,' Pia tells me. 'But it really changed things for me. I trusted what she said.'

For the first time since Raphaël died, I feel excited. *Try everything*, I remind myself. Yet there's an undertow of worry. I don't find it hard to accept that there's more to consciousness than science has discovered. It would be strange and illogical not to. But does my growing sense of a vast connectedness emerge from a broadened mind – or plain old desperation? Is my grief turning everything into a sign, a clue or a message from an invisible dimension?

Apophenia is defined as 'the tendency to perceive meaningful connections between unrelated things'. The term, coined by the psychiatrist Klaus Conrad in the 1950s, describes it as a kind of private, rolling epiphany. It troubles me that feelings which lift my heart – and which I don't want to lose by 'sobering up' – may just be symptoms of delusion. But who gets to decide what constitutes delusion? And what is best for me, as a griever? Stories offer meaning, and there's power in meaning. I want to have *more* perceptions of meaningful connections, not fewer, and I want to actively nurture the connections that my animal instinct – or my apophenia – offers me, and hone my ability to access the dimension where my child lives on: a dimension that most mediums say we have the innate capacity to reach ourselves. If the comforts of soil and sea and wildlife lift my heart more than they ever did before, and I'm starting to see the world through Raphaël's eyes as well as my own, isn't this meaningful? Aldous Huxley held that 'Knowledge is acquired when we succeed in fitting a new experience into the system of concepts based upon our old experiences. Understanding comes when we liberate ourselves from the old and so make possible a direct, unmediated contact with the new, the mystery, moment by moment, of our existence.' He is writing of a sudden shift in understanding. A change of perspective. Do our brains create thoughts, or receive them? Future Me will be glad of this, I tell myself, as I book a session later in the summer with a respected British medium. Because as Jung proclaimed, 'I shall not commit the fashionable stupidity of regarding everything I cannot explain as a fraud.'

CHAPTER 14: WILL YOU FIND RESILIENCE?

The car deck of the ferry to the island of Ærø reeks of the pigs that have just been transported to the mainland slaughterhouse. The containers bearing them are a common sight in Denmark: tall lorries with slats that reveal hints of snouts and whiskers. But the animals are always oddly silent, perhaps sensing that they're on the first and only journey of their lives. There are over twenty-five million pigs at any one time in Denmark, which has a human population of under six million. But despite being far outnumbered by another intelligent mammal, few Danes ever get to see the sentient creatures on which a big chunk of the country's agricultural economy depends, because almost all of them are intensively farmed indoors in conditions so unspeakable that cameras are effectively banned.

Born in captivity, as soon as their mothers have finished suckling them – through bars – the piglets are speed-fattened and pumped with antibiotics before being sent to slaughter in the name of cheap meat. When I was a child, the farms near my village kept pigs in outdoor enclosures dotted with corrugated iron shelters where they could sleep and rear their young in relative freedom. The end result – pork chops, mince, sausages, pet-food – was the same. But their lives were infinitely better.

Now, in an era that prides itself on being more humane and sensitive than in the past, it's a paradox that mammals and birds are kept in concentration camps and their body parts sold to consumers who are actively discouraged from connecting meat with cruelty. But in the West, the passive denialism that intensive farming promotes has deeper roots than the marketing practices of today. The medieval Great Chain of Being, which Christians believed was decreed by God, was a hierarchisation of the natural world – and a stark embodiment of human exceptionalism. God presided at the top, with his angels beneath him, and below them, man. Mammals – ranked according to their impressiveness or usefulness to humans – came lower down, and lower still came birds, reptiles, amphibians, fish, insects and crustaceans. And finally, at the very bottom, the plants and minerals upon which all the creatures above them in the hierarchy – with the exception of God and the angels – actually depend.

Up on the deck, as I breathe in the fresh air and try not to think about what goes on in the mind of a pig on its way to slaughter, Ærø's red roofs and sailing masts come into view on the horizon. In the heyday of tall ships, before the steamers came, Carsten's home town of Marstal was Denmark's second biggest port, and it still seethes with stories passed down from sailors; of the on-deck 'baptisms' for those who crossed the Equator for the first time; of smuggling; of shipwrecks off the coasts of Africa and India; of vessels trapped by ice for months near Newfoundland; of the sailors who, at sea during the German occupation, worked on allied convoy ships or fought with the British. Most of them would have felt the same visceral terror as the pigs at some point during the war, but they knew more about what was going on: knew what system they were in service to, what the conflict meant, and where they stood in the human hier-archy. They paid a high price for their courage. At the harbour there is a memorial to the eighty-four Marstallers who died – by far the highest proportion of any town in Denmark. But even in peacetime sailing was dangerous, and it was not unusual for a sailor's wife to lose her husband and all her sons. They called it the Widows' Town. As I walk the cobbled streets lined with old sailors' houses I'm newly conscious of the hard-won vitality of a commu-nity with grief in its bones and sinews; a community where loss can speak its name freely; where the ghosts of the dead still climb the rigging. How can I ever feel alone in a town where so many other women have grieved as I am grieving?

It's a fine day, with the wind stirring the ancient poplars and the sun bright on the quiet steel-blue of the Baltic. Cycling to the beach, I pass a field of horses. One is standing apart from the others, looking down at her foal, which is lying in front of her on the grass, motionless. But I swiftly dismiss the thought that comes to me so soon after passing the war memorial and smelling the terror of pigs on their way to slaughter: *Her foal is dead.* It's the thought of a grieving mother who sees a charming pastoral scene but conjures only a death.

Terns, swallows and gulls swoop and wheel above the brightly painted beach huts that form the vertebrae of the long, thin promontory known as Erik's Tail. I park my bike and pick my way along the footpath that leads through wild rose, spiky grass and clumps of sea-cabbage, past the makeshift barrier of old Christmas trees that the locals stack here every year in a heroic attempt to stall the sea's merciless encroachment. At the waterline the waves churn up pebbles, bladderwrack and broken crab shells and drag them back again in a scrim of foam that wobbles and shivers in the wind. I've come here to do something that humans have done for centuries. The stones I am looking for broke off millennia ago from parent rocks that had been ground and drilled by the relentless action of water, smaller stones or wind until they were pocked with holes. When the larger rocks broke up, their fragments rolled through time and were washed up on beaches in the form of hag stones. Rocks and stones may sit at the very bottom of the Great Chain of Being, but in many cultures they are considered to have an animus. In folklore, hag stones have the power to ward off witches, because evil spirits are too big to squeeze through the hole, while good spirits can, and do.

When I first started coming here twenty years ago, I'd be lucky to find a single hag stone in the time it took me to walk to the end of Erik's Tail and back. But when Raphaël died, that suddenly changed. The first time I came here after his death I urgently wanted to find a hag stone. 'Just lend me your eyes, Raph,' I said aloud into the wind. 'Because I need them.' He was so good at spotting animal traces: broken foliage, disturbed insect nests, hoof and claw marks, scat and dung.

He smiled. 'The trick is not to look for the stones, but for the holes,' he told me. 'When you think of a hole like that, you'll spot one. Then hold it up to the sky and look for the light.'

That day, I came back not with a single hag stone, but with fifty-four. Since then, every time I come here, I find at least thirty in the space of an hour, and often many more. And when I leave the beach with a rucksack full of stones, what I've often thought of as a metaphor for grief becomes something far more powerful: evidence of something that weighs nothing, but contains my son's presence. Most of the stones I find are small and un-assuming, and their holes are smooth. But now, where the water meets the line of seaweed, I spot a larger one: a sharp-edged black and white flintstone with a ragged hole. I pick it up and feel its chilly heft. When I hold it to the light, it re-frames the sun as a wild starburst of seething energy, and when I angle it downward, I see within the opaque moon of a stranded jellyfish the astonishing survival of a creature that has existed since the earliest eras of life on earth. Are beauty and significance something the mind creates or are they there all the time, just waiting to be noticed with a different lens?

'How many years do we all have left, Raph?' I ask.

'In Deep Time, we're just the blink of an eye.'

'Is that comforting?'

'Yes,' he says. 'It's beautiful.'

On my way home, an hour later, the mare is still standing there, and her foal is still motionless. I was right. It's dead. It could be a horrible validation. But I don't need to frame it that way. Life isn't just about what happens next or doesn't. It's about what I choose to become from what it teaches me – and what I choose to lend my thoughts to. The psychiatrist, philosopher and Holocaust survivor Viktor Frankl believed that saying yes to life means succumbing to all that death brings, and finding purpose in its wake. I can hold a hag stone in my hand and feel nothing but its cold inanimate weight. Or I can look at the grieving mare through its hole and understand that she is paying the simple price of being alive, and knowing love. Frankl held that if we had the opportunity to eliminate all our past and future emotional pain, we would say no. He believed that traumas can strengthen the psyche – which was why in his perception, some of his fellow-survivors from Auschwitz, Kaufering III, Türkheim and Theresienstadt 'left in a better, stronger state of mind' than when they entered it. I can't imagine being in a better state of mind after Raphaël's death. But I can imagine my strength returning.

'Resilience can be understood as the capacity of a system to recover from a disturbance,' writes Jeremy Lent in *The Patterning Instinct*, his exploration of how humans find and form patterns that echo the forms we are drawn to in the natural world. 'But recovery doesn't necessarily mean remaining the same; the most resilient systems are often those that are constantly adapting to changes in their environment.'

Can I become a resilient? Can I accommodate changes

and re-organise myself without losing the attributes that make me distinctively myself? Do I even want to be distinctly myself? As summer deepens and I enter the third trimester of Raphaël's transformation from alive to dead, almost despite myself I feel something in me shifting, and I remember Anaïs Nin's lines:

> And the day came when the risk to remain
> Tight in the bud was more painful than
> The risk it took to blossom.

I don't know if blossoming is what comes next for me.

But I know pain has changed me, and it will change me again, and again.

And that one day, the woman I've become will look back on the woman I was and think: I'm not less than I was before. I'm more.

CHAPTER 15: WILL THE EARTH HEAL YOU?

In prehistoric times, troglodytes lived in the cavities of the white cliffs that fringe the Lot and the smaller rivers that flow in to swell it. For centuries, people farmed the land and mined for iron ore and limestone. In wartime, the local *Résistance* camped out in the vast, labyrinthine quarry in the forest, now a sanctuary for endangered pipistrelles. This is orchard, vineyard and grove country; duck and goose country; country of cultivated maize, asparagus, tobacco, chestnuts, figs, apple, apricot and plum, where the hills and valleys exhale an ancient, mineral, vegetable energy that is different every season: sun-baked or streaked with rain, cloud-darkened or shimmering with frost, or jungled with brambles, wild rosemary and pungent gorse.

The family house is dark inside, and dank with the pervasive spore-reek of a building left empty and unheated since last autumn, when Raphaël left. He spent four months here, alone or with Kira, Savannah or groups of friends and fellow-activists, and his traces are everywhere, like an animal's: the hand-written notices outlining workshop plans and schedules, the shopping lists, the mind-maps for regeneration days and protest actions. I'm aware of tracking him, as if he's still here in all that he left behind. In the kitchen cupboard I find six jars of his home-made cherry and apricot jams, carefully labelled. On a shelf in the tool-cupboard lies the crossbow he carved as a young teenager, and something I haven't seen before: a small red silk pouch printed with Chinese characters. Inside, wrapped in newspaper and tissue, are several shards of slate. All are blank except for one. In the corner, in black pigment, he has engraved a tiny ace of spades. Somehow this is 'classic Raph'. But why the ace of spades? It comes to me that the piece of slate must be significant. I can't think why, but I decide to take it back to Denmark and add it to his shrine.

'Go outside,' says Raph, as he always does when I start to cry. It's always good advice. As children, he and Matti spent their days outdoors, shooting arrows at paper targets pinned to haybales, digging holes, mining for coloured mud, building treehouses and dens, hunting in the boggy

ditch for tadpoles, frogs and salamanders, fishing and swimming in the neighbour's lake, foraging for *cépes*, or chasing
lizards until they threw off their tails. One day we saw a
hawk drop like a stone from the sky, then rise again, a
huge snake thrashing in its talons. Back in the 1990s the
fields and hedgerows were alive with butterflies, grasshop-
pers, lizards, snakes, moles, rabbits, hares, hedgehogs and
wild flowers. But as the boys grew into men and the
effects of local agricultural pesticide spraying cascaded to
impact the species that depended on the activities of insects
and birds, every year we saw fewer of everything. The
rabbits disappeared completely, killed off by myxomatosis,
a disease intentionally – and disastrously - introduced in
France in the 1950s to control wild rabbit populations.
The birdsong became thinner, and when we ate outside
we no longer fought off the wasps, bees and flies that
once buzzed around the table at every meal. Some of our
urban visitors thought this was a blessing. But we never
did. The natural world was visibly struggling.

This tormented Raphaël. So last year, he began to rewild
our three acres of land. He asked the local farmer to stop
harvesting the grass in our field to allow it to regenerate,
and to help it along he collected and planted acorns,
walnuts, plum and cherry stones, figs and wildflower seeds.
Together, we dragged two old wicker chairs into the copse
overlooking the valley, and as we micro-dosed magic

mushrooms, the world quietly opening up in new ways, he told me more. The rabbits would come back eventually, he said: he'd already seen some healthy families up the road, near the woods. If we stopped collecting fallen branches and tree trunks in the copse and left them where they were to rot, they'd attract insect life and fungus, and nourish the soil. While the psilocybin did its subtle, revelatory work, the shriek of the cicadas intensified and there was a glossy new shimmer to the light, as if an entrance to another world had opened up, magnifying the smell of sun-baked leaf-litter, the fractal shapes of uncoiling fern leaves and the whisper of the breeze in the birch branches. We grew wildly talkative, arguing about native and non-native species, diving down rabbit-holes of speculation, and sketching nerdy maps on a huge roll of paper weighed down with stones. Watching the clouds change colour in the setting sun we became aware of another kind of energy, vivid and alive as our own blood but beyond our sensory reach: the energy of fungal threads connecting beneath the soil so the trees could send messages to one another; of seeds incubating in flowers; of spiders mating; of the invisible snaking of roots and tendrils; of the thrill of the Wild pumping through the planet's veins.

I go down to the copse where we sat and lie in the hammock he strung between two oaks – and catch my breath. Through the leaves, I spot a crazily exotic bird with a curved beak and a russet and black-and-white crest that gives its head a pickaxe shape. A hoopoe.

'Hi Raph,' I smile. It pecks at the earth for a while, then flies up onto a telephone wire, showing off the striped black-and-white feathering on its wings and tail.

Increasingly, I'm fascinated by the way birds grace and decorate the world: their jerky head-movements as they strut; their calls to one another or to the breaking day; the startling head-swivels that allow them to look at the world from any angle; the mysterious process by which they navigate their way across continents and seas; their random-looking decisions to fly from one branch to another, and then back again; how they decide to migrate after flocking and swarming in the sky; how they know where to go, and when. I want to know what it is to have wings, feathers and a gizzard. I want birds and any other creatures whose paths I cross to help me imagine what it is to be another species. And in giving me a glimpse into their worlds, recalibrate my own.

Perhaps they have already started to.

Perhaps I will cry less – and, perhaps, as the months and years go by, the rewilded land will flourish and regenerate to captivate another generation of children as it captivated mine. Perhaps there will come a time when I don't cry every day.

'I know you're here, Raph. But I need another sign. Something bigger and more difficult than a bird. Something that can't just be a coincidence.'

'Like what?'

I know immediately. An animal we only ever see in the distance, and never on our land.

'I want a deer. You've got all summer. But I want you to send me one. Here.'

It's a big ask, and I'm scared it will blow up in my face, because what if no deer comes? Still, when I get back to the house, I make Carsten my witness.

'I asked him for a deer. I told him he had all summer.'

The next afternoon two close friends who loved Raphaël join us for coffee on the wooden terrace beneath the huge oak overlooking the field. Having lost a baby of their own many years ago, his death not only devastated them but brought back their own trauma, so our meeting is as emotional as I dreaded it would be. I normally avoid telling the story of how he died, and what happened afterwards, because it's unbearable. But they need to hear it, and perhaps I need to tell it: maybe the more I do, the less jagged it will feel. By the end of it I'm crying. But Carsten, who knows me like no one else, swiftly intervenes with a Classic Raph story, and within five minutes we're all laughing, and Andy's remembering he noticed a lot of beautiful young girls around Raphaël last summer and –

He breaks off and points.

'Over there! Look!'

In front of us in the long grass no more than five metres away stands a little doe with a red-brown coat spotted with white. She's watching us, stock-still. We lock eyes, and then she turns and bounds off down the field.

Suddenly, the summer is infused with magic. What I had begun to feel and sense I now know. I've crossed a mental line.

He's here.

CHAPTER 16: WILL YOU TALK TO THE DEAD?

The living have always tried to initiate conversations with the dead. The Zoom connection is bad, so after a quick hello – I glimpse an almond face, and long blonde hair – the medium and I both switch off our video. I have told Kat Baillie that I lost a son, but nothing more, including where I am in the world: the only backdrop she can see is the staircase behind me. I'm excited at the chance to connect with Raphaël again, but there's the same bat-squeak of fear I felt when I asked for the deer. Will my sceptical self, hardwired for doubt, bully away the evidence, leaving me deflated and diminished?

But almost immediately, he has manifested. She describes a young man with long wavy hair, an 'exquisite personality', a broad, playful imagination and a sense of theatre and fun; he has a flair for writing and is in his mid-twenties. He's showing her an amazing view over fields or hills or valleys. 'He's telling me it's France,' she says. He loves it here. He's very happy in nature, and can entertain himself very easily. He feels grounded and down to earth, and he's a really good son, attentive and interested in the natural world. I confirm that all this is true. It feels both surreal and perfectly normal to be accessing him so accurately.

But then — far too suddenly and far too soon — the flow of information becomes very fast and medically specific. It's also shockingly Raph-like, as Kat flips seamlessly between 'he' and 'I', without seeming to notice the distinction. 'He's clicking his fingers for me, to say it happened just like that. It was very fast. He's talking about an erratic flutter or erratic heartbeat . . . and he's enlarging the heart slightly, swelling it up for me in my mind . . . I feel there was an underlying issue that we never knew I had. He is thankful he didn't know about it.' I'm about to confirm that one ventricle was enlarged, when Raph's torrent of information resumes. 'He's making me feel he didn't get a lot of notice, because he's snapping my fingers.' He is letting her know that he's in a group, maybe running, and when he falls people are in shock and not sure what to do. She says she feels a paramedic or military person there alongside him, and there's a jeep that came in five or ten minutes. None of this information is available on the internet.

'Now he's saying something about you influencing words on paper – have you been writing about him? I feel a book will come.' I confirm I'm writing about him. 'And now he's stroking my hand,' she says. 'When you last saw him did you stroke his hand?'

His hand, wrist and forearm flash before me. The jaguar sleeve tattoo. The freckles standing out against the paleness of his skin. The coldness of the flesh I kissed. I don't speak for a moment. It has gone very quiet in the house, as though the air has sucked itself away. There's a long silence as I fight back the tears. I can't think of a single word to say. But I don't need to, because now Raphaël is showing Kat his left wrist and shaking it to show 'wooden beads or a bracelet, maybe one of those plastic bands you get at concerts'. He was never without home-made bracelets, leather thongs, plaited strings and random bling. And now he's showing himself meditating and doing yoga. I confirm that he did both. Then he conjures an apple tree, and pulls an apple off and bites into it, looking happy. I tell her that I went to a local nursery and chose an apple tree to plant for him last week. Now he's showing her some soil and stamping his foot as if he's planted a seed. I smile, remembering everything he planted in the field. The surreal feeling continues, along-side the matter-of-factness of the information.

I ask about his brother.

'He's putting his arm over his brother's shoulder. He's looking up at him so I'm thinking it's an older brother. He's saying his brother's felt very numb and very lost and completely shocked. He doesn't want to talk about it: he wants to deal with it in his private way.' This, too, is true. She says Raphaël's brother has a partner, and his death has brought them closer: Raphaël's joining their hands together to show it's a beautiful relationship. 'They'll marry and there will be children and they'll go from strength for strength.' She stops. 'And he loves his dad. He wants to express his love to him. And his respect. He knows he's really hurting and it's really shocked him. Now – oh. I've got a fishing feeling coming in: is there a fishing connection?'

Yes. The three of them often fished together when the boys were young. On their last holiday together last summer, they fished again.

Now an older man appears, and he's showing her his hands. 'That means he's a practical man. Creative. Does he make furniture or was that his trade? He's started to fix a chair. He says you're the love of his life.'

I laugh. My father became a violin-maker when I was twelve, but before that he was a carpenter. And there wasn't a single chair in my childhood home that he hadn't either made or mended.

I'm left astounded, yet not completely surprised. Of course my father is there, and of course Raphaël appeared. Why wouldn't both the dead people I love most be emphatically present? The way the medium so effortlessly embodied Raphaël's personality; his connection with France; his description of how he died; the bracelets on his wrist; the apple tree; the seeds he planted; the meditation and the yoga; the nature of his brother's and father's grief; the fact that they went fishing, and that my father worked with his hands: it all feels conclusive.

Kierkegaard wrote: 'There are two ways to be fooled. One is to believe what isn't true; the other is to refuse to believe what is.'

And I am no refuser.

An hour later, I am still digesting Raphaël's visit when Matti and Piluca arrive, bearing gifts of cheese and ham and wine. They are radiant. Bereavement and the pandemic have fused them into a single unit, and I can tell at a glance that the last few gruelling months have intensified their love.

Perhaps Raph is right that they will marry and have children. How good it is to have a son-hug again. To have a living, breathing, laughing, funny, quick-witted, kind, handsome flesh-and-blood son, brimming with energy and love.

'You'll never guess what just happened,' I tell them. And out it pours.

Matti has brought a pot-plant with him all the way from Germany: a spekboom grown from a cutting I took in South Africa, on an impulse, in the hope that something from that place of trauma might flourish and offer some kind of consolation for the horror we'd been through. He stands the pot on the low wall of the veranda and I watch him spritz the succulent with water, check its leaves and note its new shoots. We talk about how it's flourishing, but we don't talk about the fact that it symbolises his brother, and the wild world he loved, and that by tending to it, Matti is tending to him in the only way he can. There's no need to.

Later, we walk through a steep wooded slope dotted with crimson fungi that are latticed like tiny cages, and bright and shiny as plastic toys. At the foot of the cliff studded with metal hooks, Matti and Piluca put on their climbing gear and take turns to navigate the rock face, feeding one another slack and calling out suggestions about where to put their hands or feet. I've tried to hide my fear that Matti will fall to his death, but he knows it's there, and I know this trip is his attempt to reassure me. It flashes through my mind that now is when it will happen, and I'll see my son falling from the sky to his death. But I slap the fear down and relax into the pleasure of seeing them climb, and as I watch them feed the rope to one another, I'm reassured. Matti won't die in my lifetime.

An hour later, he hands me a harness.

'OK, Ma. Your turn.'

He's right. It's not enough to see their safety. I need to feel it. As I put on the harness and assess the cliff's ridges, fissures, bumps and hand-holds, I'm gripped by a sudden, primal urge. I don't just want to climb: I need to.

I take it fast, and as I navigate the rock face, it's my body making the decisions, not my brain. As a child I loved scaling rocks and climbing trees. It's an instinct as deep as apehood.

I love it. I am even good at it. Matti's hunch was right. The fear is gone.

I'm free.

CHAPTER 17: WHEN THE WILD CALLS YOU, WILL YOU ANSWER?

Every summer in France, I rediscover wildness. But this year I am hungrier for it than ever before, because I'm seeing it with two sets of eyes: Raphaël's and mine. The more I wander on the land and the more time I spend swinging in the hammock in the copse, the more I realise how huge my hunger for wildness had grown in our fourth-floor apartment in Copenhagen: how extensive the creep of my nature deficit disorder. Among these hills, I appreciate every unfurling shoot, every thundercloud, every bird-call, every anthill, every toadstool, every frog-croak, every grape, every spiderweb, every black-eyed daisy, every trail of snail-slime.

My musician niece Anna, who has come to stay from Paris, feels it too. We're sitting in a copse of beech and young oak trees next to the moss-covered stone that Matti has placed in Raphaël's memory. I've planted ferns and sage and lavender around it, and when friends and family visit, they place a smaller stone on it to mark their visit, as our Jewish ancestors did when honouring their dead. Like my little bookshelf shrine in Copenhagen, the stone is a grave without being a grave: a place to visit Raphaël, and talk to him. As the heat lifts and the light begins to fade, I lie in his hammock and Anna sits on a faded wicker seat. Not long after Raphaël died, she tells me, she took a psychedelic drug which is similar to the Peruvian hallu-cinogen ayahuasca, but with a shorter high of only fifteen minutes. It was her first time, and it was a bad trip – 'a bit like an NDE, maybe, but a scary one' – and she was terrified. 'But then Raphaël appeared and he calmed me down, and he stayed with me the whole time, till I came out of it.'

I smile in gratitude. Of course he came to help her.

I tell Anna about the signs that Raph has sent, and she tells me about her asthmatic friend who died of Covid just a month after he did, and about her music-festival group, the Glowy Owls. By now it's dark and we can barely see each other. But the white shape that suddenly floats through a gap in the trees and circles silently around us is utterly clear. A barn owl. It does another circuit and then flies off again into the darkness. I've never seen one here before. Anna bursts into laughter. 'That was him,' she says. 'Since he died I've been seeing owls everywhere.' Then a further surprise: as we walk back in the darkness, our way is suddenly lit by a single pinprick of intense light: a glow-worm. And Anna's celebrating all over again. 'First he sent the owl, and then he sent the glow.'

The episode confirms the intuition that has brought me this far: an intuition that unites me with all the others who stumble along the ill-lit path that leads to a gentler, lighter understanding of the world; an understanding you could call meaning. My intimation of what lies beyond the known world of our five senses doesn't feel like sentimentality, or magical thinking, or an elaborate delusionary system born of pattern-making – though it may turn out to be any or all of these things. It feels real and important in the same way that scientific understanding and creative inspiration feel real and important. They don't need to be mutually exclusive. If I were a scientist, I might know how to go about testing the limits of consciousness. But I already know that when I'm writing fiction, there is often a moment when an unexpected thought or image appears from nowhere. Once, my first urge was to bat it away as an intrusive mental curveball. But I have learned to follow it and ask it what it wants. And again and again such moments have proved an unexpected gift, containing the beating heart of the story I'm working on. I have a growing sense that these insights are shared property: gifts from an energetic dimension available to us all, beyond the limits of the known. So my instinct now is to give in to bewilderment, and to admit that what I deemed as fixed and certain no longer is: to relinquish the web of connections, built over years of education and experience, that formed my belief system, to give way to uncertainty and ambiguity, and to be humble enough to say I don't know any more, and that's OK.

The slew of validations in such a short space of time, in the place Raph loved best in the world, reinforces my conviction that he's actively around us. What if the nature of this dimension – surely one of many – is just one of those as-yet undiscovered and unproven unknowns? Maybe life is the dream that death wakes us from. Sometimes I sense him hovering near my skin.

If he is, then he is telling me I can do this. And this summer has taught me that I can.

PART FOUR: AUTUMN
AND WINTER

CHAPTER 18: WILL YOU KNOW WHERE YOU ARE HEADED?

The mountains are dark and jagged in the distance, their peaks shrouded in cloud. The air, tinged with the fungal smell of autumn, is cooling as we travel north, past harvested fields fringed by late-fruiting bushes and yellowing trees. Soon the birds will be migrating.

Journeys are a kind of limbo. In it, we are everyone and nobody, and more invisible than we have ever been to the world – but also to ourselves. As the kilometres pass, the summer evaporates, and on we move. But it's not the same as moving on. 'To tell someone with a dead child, "you should move on", is doubly thoughtless, because there is no medium left through which to move anywhere,' writes the poet Denise Riley, whose son died as suddenly as Raphaël did. 'If there is ever to be any movement again that moving will not be "on" it will be "with". With the carried-again child.'

I picture Raphaël on the back seat, as a young boy. 'When are we going to be there?'

I reply as I always replied on long car trips. 'Soon.'

But I don't know what I'm talking about. I don't even know where we're really headed. There are no signposts, and ours isn't the kind of journey that ends. All I know, for now, is that I'm curious about the new turns it will take, and how much of what I've learned I'll carry with me.

On the car radio we hear reports of fires spreading from California to the East Coast, flash floods in Afghanistan, and oil companies planning to drill the Arctic. I'm increasingly aware of how my grief for Raphaël is enmeshed with a more inchoate grief for all the intricately interconnected and mutually dependent species and wildlife habitats the world is losing. By 2050, the giant panda, the blue whale, the hawksbill turtle, the river dolphin, the African lion, the Bornean orangutan, the South China tiger, the rhinoceros, the Indian vulture, the polar bear, the red tuna, the gorilla and krill, the food of whales, are highly likely to be extinct. But no coastline, no coral reef, no forest, no mammal, no glacier, and no species of plant, insect, water creature or bird lives or dies in a vacuum. Every loss brings a cascade of consequences. To be aware of this is to feel the anticipatory grief known by those who love someone who is dying, or whose life is shadowed by illness, depression or addiction. And it brings an existential dread.

But grief isn't the end of any story. Instead, I am beginning to frame it as a portal to the wider consciousness that all of humankind once knew: a deep, embodied sense of the intricate web of symbiotic structures that sustains every species on the planet. Raphaël always had this knowledge in his bloodstream. And even though he's physically gone, it feels like he's still part of this web. Because how could he ever leave it?

Outside our apartment block in Copenhagen, our guerrilla garden is a wild chaos of hollyhocks past their prime, papery irises, straggling cosmos, and a rash of fat hen, the edible weed that thrives in poor soil, and is among the first to sprout from rubble. Upstairs, I head for the balcony and throw myself into re-potting and re-planting. I put seeds in the bird-feeder in the hope that through simple continuities – feeding the birds, meditating, taking morning swims, talking to Raph, and writing this story – I can continue too.

When Matti calls to say that his heart tests – delayed by the pandemic – are negative, the relief rushes through me, stealing my breath and bringing me close to tears.

'I never thought you had it,' I tell him.

'Nor did I.' The silent subtext is that we were so scared we couldn't name it. But now we're on a high. We talk about his climbing, and my morning swims. How for both of us, since Raphaël died, our physicality has taken on a new dimension and become a vital part of healing.

I feel my true needs in the water, without being able to name them or even wanting to. It's sometimes glassy, sometimes rough. Some days the level is lower, revealing clusters of mussels clinging to the pier-struts, and sometimes so high that my hair brushes the slats of the wooden bridge leading to the pontoon as I swim beneath it. Sometimes it's dense, like a viscous soup. Other days it's light and silky as a caul. Seabirds fly overhead: gulls, cormorants, swans, ducks and Arctic terns. When one of them squawks, it's Raphaël, urging me on.

Keep doing this, he says.

And I tell him that I will.

Keep doing everything, he says. *And then do more.*

Despite myself, I have been. Over the summer, Carsten and I offered to organise a literary event to coincide with Extinction Rebellion Denmark's September protest, at which both of us will speak. It will be my first time in a crowd since Raphaël died, and my first attempt at speaking publicly.

After seven months of being a recluse, I feel raw and vulnerable, standing on a soapbox in front of a crowd of

200 in the freezing wind. But I need to do this. For Raph, and for me. I tell the crowd how grief can do two things: it can shrink your soul – or it can expand it. The wind is fierce, the microphone is dodgy, and the hardest part is coming, the part where I talk about Iggy Fox, and the solace of knowing that the heart that stopped beating at the age of twenty-five was a committed one. As I speak, I'm aware of his energy in me, and it gives me strength. I end by quoting from the defence statement he wrote after vandalising the Brazilian Embassy in London:

> As scientists we're taught to be impartial. Our job is to observe reality, collect the data, analyse the results, and report the facts – to tell the cold, hard, mathematical truth. But what do you do when that truth is so horrific it keeps you awake at night? What do you do when the results of observed reality are so inhumane that your inaction becomes a moral wrong?

As a huge cheer erupts from the throng in front of me, I feel Raph's smile breaking out on my face. Perhaps the fact that he is dead needn't change things as radically as I thought. Because when I stood up and spoke, we spoke together.

It was a watershed, I think afterwards. I feel lighter. Buoyant, even. Raphaël was right that activism is an antidote to depression. When I start to join Writers Rebel Zoom meetings again, I feel a zing of my old energy. But the undertow of fear remains, and as Raph's birthday approaches the dread returns. I know from other bereaved parents that the first anniversaries without your child are the hardest to bear. I know, too, that when your child dies, he drops out of time. Birthdays don't mean anything to the dead. But I can't ignore September 30, and I don't want to: I want to celebrate it. To celebrate *him*. But how?

In Yoko Ogawa's short story 'Afternoon at the Bakery', the narrator visits a bakery to buy two strawberry short-breads. There's nobody serving in the shop, and only one other customer, an older woman, who approves of her decision to buy the shortcakes: they're very good. They strike up a conversation.

'I'm buying them for my son,' says the narrator. 'Today is his birthday.'

'Really?' says the old woman. 'Well I hope he has a happy one. How old is he?'

'Six,' she replies. 'He'll always be six. He's dead.'

On the morning of September 30th, Carsten presents me with a little *musvit* carved from wood. I stand it on the table, and together we wish Raphaël a happy birthday, and then we're crying. Over the course of the day, many people send messages telling me how they're holding their own rituals – in South American jungles, at animal rescue centres, on mountaintops, in London pubs or simply cocooning at home, remembering their own private versions of the Wild. In the evening I reproduce the vegan pizzas we made together on Raphaël's last visit, and we drink cocktails over a Zoom with family. We are all dressed up for the occasion and everyone makes the effort to laugh and not cry, because it's what he'd want. But it exhausts me.

As the autumn days begin to darken, and my morning swims get colder, I feel I'm taking one step forward and two steps back. My chronic sleeplessness returns, and I lie in bed unable to tell where one kind of sadness ends and another begins, or whether it's all just one vast sadness that will go on and on.

'Raph's dead,' I say aloud, for the thousandth time – as if I need reminding. But the word dead has begun to rankle. I need another one.

'Try disembodied,' he suggests.

So I try it. 'Raph's disembodied.'

Sometimes, I manage disembodiment too. When I sit to meditate, I become blind and silent, and deaf to my own breathing. Then, dissolving into energy, I travel as far as my imagination will take me, and then let its waves carry me further. And in the dimension that's just a breath away, in the vast spaciousness that encompasses everything, I feel his presence.

CHAPTER 19: WILL YOU BELIEVE IN THE POSSIBLE?

'Fox saw the potential and the best in us before we recognised it ourselves,' a friend of Raphaël writes to me. 'He believed in what was not yet possible. But he believed in it as if it had already happened: as if it was already there.' We are all born with an imagination. So how hard can it be to use that gift to re-frame the difficult as the achievable, and the achievable as the future? Because of the nature of news, which necessarily focuses on negative disruption, the trajectory of world history is enough to terrify anybody. But every day there's proof that trajectories can change. The European Union and seventy-two countries from all regions of the world have made a pledge to reverse biodiversity loss by 2030. A project has been launched to plant twenty-five million trees across Australia in the wake of the bushfires. After fifty years of effort, six and a half million acres of indigenous land in Canada's Northwest Territories is now officially protected.

'One story I frequently encounter frames the possibilities in absolutes: if we can't win everything, then we lose everything,' writes Rebecca Solnit. She attributes this to a narrative failure: 'the inability to imagine a world different than the one we currently inhabit'. In *A Paradise Built in Hell* she writes about how, in the immediate wake of Hurricane Katrina, 'elite panic' took over, and the disaster became a socio-political catastrophe exacerbated by the authorities themselves. But the purpose of her book is to show how again and again, throughout history, ordinary citizens caught in disasters of every kind tend to cooperate heroically, and often risk their own lives in acts of altruism. In emergency situations, shock and grief do not generally cause people to behave antisocially – but institutionalised opportunism does. And in the wake of any disaster, the biggest opportunists are those in power. When they fear they may lose that power, and that the growth economy will be jeopardised, they concentrate their energies on locking it down and fortifying it further.

Now, as the planet's crisis deepens, with temperatures rising, tipping points being breached, and epidemiologists warning that the Covid pandemic is just a taste of pandemics to come, I wonder how the competing tendencies to cooperate and to grab or maintain power will play out on a global scale when things really fall apart. The eco-philosopher Joanna Macy uses the analogy of the bardo to delineate the extremities we are likely to reach before systemic change becomes possible. She considers it inevitable that climate and ecological breakdown will lead to global economic and social collapse within decades. But as with grief, the way out is through. She posits three versions of reality that are already shaping the way ahead. The first – the 'marching order' of governments, the military, publicly traded corporations and the corporate-controlled media – is Business as Usual. The second she calls The Great Unravelling, because with the collapse of living structures caused by the commodification of the natural world, systems fray, precipitating the long, fraught endgame.

But it's not quite the endgame, because there is a third story, in which salvation may yet lie: a transition to a life-sustaining society. Comparable to the agricultural and industrial revolutions in its magnitude and scope, this ecological revolution – The Great Turning – emerges after we have 'survived' the earlier stories and are open to becoming a society that honours its debt to the future of not just our own species, but to all the planet's inhabitants.

It is that story that Raphaël chose, embodied and helped

to tell. He knew that enough small acts of vision, compassion and integrity, working together, can amass like snowflakes to precipitate an avalanche.

Here is where Raphaël's belief in a liveable future lay, and where mine does too. And as the season deepens, an image is crystallising: an image of my body letting him go, and my own emergence from a time of darkness.

CHAPTER 20: WILL YOU GIVE AND RECEIVE GIFTS?

The season has fully turned again, and the trees are bare against the red rooftops of Marstal. I always dread the brutal, fog-bound weeks of midwinter, when the sun doesn't rise till nine and is setting by three. But this year, now that the worst imaginable thing has happened, there is nothing left to dread – leaving me to experience the months ahead as animals do: as a time of hibernation and withdrawal in which I store up energy and await the sun's return.

Most pregnancies end happily. I can't see how my phantom version will, and I don't know what to expect, beyond the closing of a crazy chapter that began to write itself after Raphaël died. But today, on November 6th, nine months on, my metaphor must finish its work and

I must trust it. I light a candle, swallow a pinch of his ashes, and lie on the bed with his baby blanket, his lock of hair and my wooden *musvit*. I clutch my belly and convulse. I'm not ready to let him go but I can't stop it: I came up with the metaphor and now it's obeying my logic.

He's at my side and holding my hand as I breathe.

'Give me a sign, Raph.'

The candle, which has been flickering madly, stops. The flame is still.

After a moment it starts flickering again as suddenly as it stopped. I don't trust my eyes.

'Do it again, Raph.'

And it stops the flickering again, and I see his face in the pattern of roses on the candle. His eyes are closed in rapture. It's him. And then it flickers again and I say, 'Do it one more time' – and he does it again.

Time passes, and I convulse again, as if every last cell of him as an embodied person must be expelled. I may have brought it on psychosomatically, but the pain feels real enough, and as I clutch my belly I feel the metaphor I have conjured doing its job: to embody my acceptance of his death, and to manifest my own re-birthing. It comes to me that all lives and all deaths are part of an exchange within a wider web of energy – like the synapses that fire within the brain's neural networks, like the servers and nodes of the internet that connect the world of thought, like the underground fungal systems that unite whole forests, like the complex symbiosis of marine biology on a coral reef. I am part of the life that depends on all the other life: part of a connective force whose movement is so dynamic that it is not so much a noun as a verb, like combustion, like vibration, like expansion, like the movement of air or water, or the thrust of organic growth.

The next morning, I swim across the harbour towards the jetty where the ferries dock. A pink dawn is breaking on the horizon and I'm the only human here. The water – glassy, freezing – burns my skin as I move through it, and my breath comes out in clouds. It's beautiful. I am a creature swimming and breathing, free of thought. Suddenly, just as I'm turning to swim back, a small bird with a grey coat and a bright blue breast swoops low in the water, almost close enough to touch. It traces a wide arc right in front of me. Then it squawks loudly and flies off. I whirl around in time to see it vanish.

I burst into laughter.

So unlikely. And so classically Raph, to squawk right in my face to make me laugh.

'Raph!' I yell into the dawn. 'It was you! I know it!'

Back home, shivering but elated, I look up Baltic seabirds.

No small bird with grey plumage and a bright blue breast exists in the Baltic. Or anywhere else, that I can see.

Somehow, this is no surprise.

But I saw it. It was there.

I booked the table months ago, if only to be able to say that we celebrated my birthday in a way Raphaël would have wanted. He loved giving presents. He was famous for them. The best were always home-made, and theatrical, like the peacock-feather earrings he made for a girlfriend, or the rings he carved in jungle camps from coconut shells, or the filigree necklace he made for me, with a single green stone embedded in it, that I'm wearing now. I'd like to have taken him to this exclusive place, hidden in a semi-industrial no-man's-land and renowned for its mind-bendingly experimental food.

But it turns out he's here already. As we settle at our table I slip my little wooden *musvit* out of my handbag and place it in front of me. Our waitress arrives and introduces herself. I don't catch her name, but her accent is Dutch. She's about to talk us through the woodland-themed menu when her eye falls on my *musvit* and she stops short.

'That's my bird,' she says. There's a confused pause.

'Your bird, how?' I ask. 'Because it's actually mine.'

'It's a *maise*. That's my name. It means great tit in Dutch.' We look at one another in elated astonishment. Maise says she is used to people laughing at her name, especially English people: the double meaning amuses them. But I explain that we're actually laughing because the great tit is someone else's bird, too: someone who couldn't be here. And that's why he's sitting on the table. I don't need to say another word: Maise gets it immediately, and is discreet enough to ask no more. Instead, she rolls up the sleeves of her black shirt to show us the tattoos on her forearms. Two *musvits*.

When Maise has left us, we raise a toast to Raphaël. That's our boy, we say. Tonight, he pulled out the stops. But he isn't done. When the sommelier arrives with a new bottle of wine, I read the label and flash back to the little shard of green-grey stone, engraved in black, that I found among Raphaël's things in France. I'd felt that it had to appear again. And now here it is.

The name of the wine is Ace of Spades. Two clear signs, on my birthday.

Later it will cross my mind to google the meaning of the ace of spades, which I will learn is also known as 'the Death Card'. But for now, I'm unaware of the darker significance of the unwitting *momento mori* his fingers conjured in an idle moment, and left forgotten in a red silk pouch on a shelf in France.

The meal finished, we wander back into the darkness of a Danish winter night. It's been an intimate, fragile, tender evening, filled with the sense that Raphaël was with us, enjoying every smell and taste, and joining in the laughter. I know that the memory of it will be a source of gratitude and grace to draw on when darkness descends again. That I'll look back on this evening and smile at Raph's panache.

The darkness will return, I know – but I'm stronger than I was.

And this evening has made me stronger still.

The ocean defies the land. Its rhythm is the moon, and the inhalation and exhalation of the tide. It's as plain and vast and sacred as the sky. Immersed in the quiet, low-brine Baltic, there's freedom. My attention is on nothing but my movement through the dak morning water: the insistent physical now-ness of the moment. It's time out of the normal rhythm of life, time in another realm, my warm-bloodedness against the sea's iciness a reminder that only a membrane divides us. I'm part of the gloaming that precedes the sunrise; part of the wind turbines turning on the horizon and the sleeping apartment blocks; of fish, weed, mussels and the jellyfish that bump softly against my skin, a tiny nudge from an alien world. In these moments I am a soul in a body, a body alive with bone, organs, blood and muscle; a body whose heart still beats and whose lungs still fill with air, a body that may one day learn to feel joy as well as grief. Sometimes I imagine Raphaël swimming deep beneath me, shadowing my progress and keeping me company. Even though he has no breath to hold, he holds it, as if he might just torpedo up from the water in front of me, laughing, saltwater shooting off him, his braided hair a long, wet rope.

The cold cuts deeper with every swim, but once my body knows it's staying submerged for perhaps longer than it would like, perhaps long enough to die if I wanted it to, the shock melts away, and it liberates itself from all presuppositions about what it can tolerate. My mind does the same. When I swim, its relentless chatter ceases. I used to think that winter sea-swimmers were mad, but now I know that, like me, they are keeping sane. Instead of fighting the discomfort I embrace it, and feel it balance me. One day, emerging, I'm shocked to see blood pouring from a huge graze on my thigh where I must have scraped my skin on ice. I never felt it happening because I was desensitised by cold, and on my return home I still don't feel it. I never feel it, though the scar is there for days.

The idea that my metabolism has changed to cope with sub-zero temperatures and low-level hypothermia is exciting to me. The colder it gets, the more I want to test my limits. I swim in fog and snow and hail. When there's pancake ice, I swim around the bobbing plates. When the surface is frozen, I smash the brittle film, and when it's too thick to breach, I find a place where someone as deranged as me has melted a hole, and swim in circles.

I am always strangely euphoric when I emerge salt-wet into the drab cityscape, with its cafes and its supermarkets and its bicycles and trains, sometimes to air so cold that when I strip off my swimsuit it freezes itself to the jetty's wooden slats, and I must crack it off. I did it and survived. I even thrived. I plunged my soul into the freezing water. If nothing else, I did this single, simple, precious thing today: I lived as the animal I am. I felt my creaturehood. It doesn't surprise me that there's increasing scientific evidence of the physical and mental benefits of regular, low-level hypothermia, but my own experience is all the proof I need.

My grief is a live, muscled, raucous being. But when I swim, it is stilled by the other creature inside me: the one that feels only the urgency of the present moment, sensing that if I didn't swim in cold water every day my soul could drown. My daily plunges have a primal, instinctive quality, and the euphoria they bring is the best antidote to grief I know. Part of this antidote is to do with the clear corollary between cold swimming and misery. It's as if my freezing plunges and my grief operate in parallel. One is physical, the other mental. One is a choice, the other isn't. But both are tests. If I can endure freezing water, I can endure losing my son. If I can endure losing my son, I can endure freezing water. Each reinforces the other with a vibrant, subterranean energy, and embodies the extremity of what I can and must do to stay alive. My system — by which I mean brain, blood, mind, viscera, soul, bones, the whole package — seems to know that the not-killing of me will make me strong.

In the process of grieving, I have changed. Metamorphosis is too big a word, perhaps. But during my nine months in this terrifying shadowland, I feel I have reached a deeper understanding of what it is to be alive on this planet at a time when there is so much that must be done, at speed, and so little political will to do it, yet a deep, collective yearning among ordinary people — powerless individually but potent as a force — to save what can be saved.

I know that I can make tiny steps back into the world — a bruised and threatened world, but the one I will live in until my death. That I mustn't waste this time, and I must dwell on what works: on my friendships and my family; on activism, on the soil, the sky, the water — and my journey back into life.

Like so many others hollowed out by sorrow, I have persisted: in breathing, in not succumbing to despair, in taking joy in life wherever I can find it. A hole is not a vacancy, but a new aperture through which to see the world. It's a small invisible shift of perception, but it feels sacred. More, I have come to believe that my future doesn't have to be a downward spiral. That there can be explosions of laughter, small pleasures and delights, and great sky-flashes of joy. That instead of being a deeply grieving human who is sometimes happy I can be a happy human who sometimes feels deep grief.

Online, I come across a picture of a hermit crab that has set up home inside the head of a plastic doll. Is this normal? Natural? To the crab, it is both. Perhaps we are becoming that crab. Not everyone feels ready to acknowledge the growing unhomeliness. Many actively resist it. But the collective consciousness of our species has never been idle.

We can build new myths, new stories, that encompass both the ruined skyscrapers of modernity and the ruins of our ancient forebears. In *The Good Ancestor: A Radical Prescription for Long-Term Thinking*, Roman Krznaric evokes the question posed by Jonas Salk, who developed the polio vaccine and refused to patent it on the grounds that it should be available to all, for the common good: 'Are we being good ancestors?' At the moment, Krznaric argues, the future of today's young and the coming generations has been effectively colonised by the political and economic paradigms of today. But if we can bring about what he calls ecological civilisation, then one day the glaciologist's son can tell his young daughter: 'Once upon a time, our compassion, foresight and ingenuity saved us from the brink. When we learned to love the Earth again, it loved us back.'

Question One: What if we can't manage it in time?

Question Two: What can we do to make it happen?

Question Three: If you could only ask Question One or Question Two, which would you choose?

CHAPTER 21: WILL YOU WRITE STORIES?

All January, I have been getting heart palpitations, and Carsten is visited by a debilitating headache every afternoon. The Death Day is haunting us.

Our symptoms intensify as February approaches, coupled with anxiety about the fate of the XR activists who are tunnelling under London's Euston Square to save its ancient trees, threatened by a costly and deluded high-speed rail project. Some of the protesters are Raph's very closest friends, and I know that if he were alive today, he'd be down there with them. Some of them say they can feel his presence as they dig like foxes to stop the advance of the rail construction. But their safety worries me. There are reports that the tunnels are in danger of collapsing. I don't want other young lives to be lost, and

I don't believe Raphaël would either. But I know why they are doing it. Once you know the stakes, you can't go back. In this context, action – whether it succeeds or fails – becomes an imperative.

When the day comes, I mark it by sending out a short film I have been working on. The words consist of a passage from Raph's notebook, read by young people who were close to him. When I first came across it, what struck me most forcibly was that it contained another premonition of his early death. But that wasn't the thrust of his message. Savannah is the last to appear in the film, speaking his final words from the heart of the dark, cramped tunnel under Euston Square.

My entire being now revolves around what we do.

Nothing has ever inspired me so powerfully. Nothing has ever given me so much hope or such a sense of purpose. Nothing has ever been so clear to me as these visions that I have for the future. I call them visions, because unlike hope or dreams they feel solid, tangible, traceable, catchable, possible, achievable – reality in the making.

I'm not foolish enough to think that this can be done alone. While people are the source of the endless destruction I hope to put a stop to, they are also the key to reaching our goals.

So spark, shelter, and nurture the flame of passion until it roars. That energy, that power, can be harnessed to change the world.

So let these legs push me to where I am needed. Let these arms pull the weight that must be shifted. Let these hands make what needs to be created. Let these eyes find the world's beauty and let these ears listen to its song and let this mind see its truth and to inspire others.

I wonder how long it will take, or if we'll ever get there. Perhaps we'll reach this brave new world in a decade, perhaps we'll still be moving towards that long after I'm dead. But remembering my nickname and looking in the mirror at Icarus's wing tattooed on my shoulder, I know it doesn't matter whether I'm here or gone. What matters is that we keep moving on and on until we get there. My wings may melt, but the rest of you will reach your destination. When the light leaves my eyes, and I pass on, do not weep for me, for I am not dead. All that I ever was and ever will be lies in the flame of passion that consumed me, the same flame that burns in all those who believe in what I believed.

I'll not be dead until my dream is, I'll not fade away until my vision does, I'll not be gone until all my hopes are.

We watch it, and we cry. But there's pride too. We have risen to the occasion. We've honoured the day.

As the film is shared and the messages pour in, I feel elated that he has spoken to the world again, and relieved that the day we've dreaded has been redeemed with such grace. But most of all I'm grateful that we had Raphaël with us for as long as we did. And that he's still with us.

That night, in London, there's a livestreamed vigil to honour the activists who have dug themselves underground to stop the felling of trees in Euston Square. And because the tunnellers dedicated their action to him, the vigil is in Raph's honour too. I join them online. There are Fox stories, and speeches, and prayers, and a hauntingly pure song from his friend Amy, who says simply: 'He helped me find my voice.'

Afterwards, Kira sends me some images of a beautiful fox, its fur stark against the white snow. It appeared when she was walking with friends in the woods. The fox showed no fear: it came up close to her and her friends. She knew, without doubt, that it was him.

I remember asking, soon after Raphaël died, while holding a pomegranate in a supermarket: does he have to be dead every day? Couldn't he be alive again just one day a year? One minute, even?

Today that wish felt granted.

Dates matter. The reverse pregnancy metaphor, I realise,

was about imposing order on my mental chaos by suggesting a structure for my grief, built around a period of three trimesters after which a new version of myself might come into being, and learn to flourish. It worked because I am suggestible in the way we all are, as members of a storytelling species. 'Stories are the means by which we understand, rationalise and moralise change,' Raphaël wrote. 'Tell the right ones now, and we can make a brighter future.'

Status quos feel permanent, but they never are. They are prone to rapid change, and never more so than in times of crisis, when we are forced to imagine and embody other ways of being, as I was. So perhaps this kairos era in ecological and climate history – a time of disasters and upheavals that will kill millions and displace billions – is one humankind will one day look back on as a civilisational Near-Death Experience from which it returned transformed.

A new belief system is growing inside me like a coral reef. My sense that the non-human world has its own vast orchestra of voices is new to me, but it's more ancient than humankind. Raphaël, who grew up as a creature of the earth, knew that it is only in embracing our creaturehood again that humankind can find its place, and its peace. The fact that this is achievable through a collective cognitive shift convinces me that there can be far more to this era than collapse and chaos. Within every disaster there is massive, transcendent opportunity. It is a uniquely thrilling time to be alive.

There is fierce life in grief. Warped, unwelcome life but vibrating with energy just the same, insisting on its right to be. If there was no love in grief, there would be no grief. Grief needs tenderness. It's all too easy to dismiss it as the self-pity that closes its doors on everything beyond one's own skin. But self-pity is one thing, and self-compassion is another. The love that's still there when the object of your love has died can't be ignored and nor should it. I hope you feel this now. When it's tormenting me most I try to give it the space it insists on – not because I want to wallow in it, but because if I plunge my soul in its freezing waters every day and don't deny its terrifying force, then I can trust that strength will come: the strength that the body summons, the strength that reminds me that the human spirit, like the body, can survive the worst of hardships and emerge renewed. The last thing Raphaël would want me to do is to squander the time I have left. But the hours and days and months I have spent grieving have served their purpose in teaching me that I can emerge from this season of devastation more fully alive and with a mind more spacious than when I entered it. Grief is a condition of our collective existence. To live fully, we must suffer rejections, tortures, bafflements, shames and disappointments alongside what happiness we find, or make. To live fully, we must know grief as well as joy; frustration as well as surprise; bewilderment as well as certainty. But most of all, we must know and embody love.

Shakespeare never saw a coral reef, but he intuited the exquisite intricacy of a marine ecosystem in which thousands of mutualistic relationships thrive in constant, regenerative flux. When the dead father's eyes in *The Tempest* become pearls, the image encapsulates the astonishing processes by which one thing becomes another. Raphaël and I and all who loved him have undergone precisely this: a sea-change. A transmutation. His is more radical than mine. I see him in the natural world because he was always curious about it, always in love with it, and always at one with it. There's a melancholy sweetness in knowing that he can go anywhere and be anything he wants to now. He can be a ginko leaf, a stingray, a bat, a tiger, a spider, a sea-turtle, a viper, a jellyfish, a droplet of water in a cloud, a bed of moss, a bacteria, an elephant, a dragonfly. He can shape-shift, he can swim in the deepest oceans, burrow to the centre of the earth, fly without wings, somersault between stars and galaxies.

The ancient meaning of 'apocalypse' connotes revelation and unveiling. If the turbulent third decade of the third millennium is a foretaste of the bigger, broader disasters to come, it is doing its work by unveiling our intercon-nectedness, highlighting the limitations of the Earth's resources, and inviting us back to the home so many of us left when we grew up, or barely ever knew: the natural world. For now – but not for ever – we have fallen out of alignment with our home, the nest and crucible of all we are. We forgot how to nurture it and now we're wondering why it isn't nurturing us back. But it's not too late. It never is. As Lao Tzu said: 'When I let go of what I am, I become what I might be.' Our civilisation has taken thousands of years to reach this point. For most of that time, clean water, unpolluted air, healthy soil and liveable temperatures were a given. Had societies consistently invested in the long-term wellbeing of their populations, we would not be facing an existential crisis. Our leaders may have failed us, but it's not the end. It's a becoming.

There is power in the cognitive dissonance the clima-tologist spoke about: in holding two belief systems, or two sets of knowledge, that are at odds. There is space in all of us for grief over all we are losing, and for trust in a liveable future. The fact that we all house paradoxes is evidence of a flexibility that could take us forward into a new understanding. I don't know what that may look like, yet. But just as I believe that a new kind of life is taking root in me as a result of Raph's death, so I believe the intensification of global turmoil is part of the great crack that will let the light in and wake us up. But even more, I believe it will come to re-awaken an ancient consciousness that was once universal, a vitalist under-standing that we are dependent on the healthy flourishing of the great, wild organism that sustains us.

As for my own metamorphosis, it has opened my mind to a dimension I wasn't aware of before. It wasn't superstition that brought me here, or religion, or even the Wild, but the surprising, continued presence of my son. I realised that if you love the dead, they'll love you back.

It could be that I will 'come to my senses' and look back on the year Raphaël died as one of interesting proof of how a broken heart can conjure what it needs to mend. A year in which my magical thinking got the better of me and scrambled my synapses. Or simply a year in which my creaturely survival instinct kicked in and I did what other organisms do in the face of catastrophe: adapt or die. But that hasn't happened yet, and I don't believe it will. And if coming to my senses means losing my new awareness of a dimension that exists in parallel to ours, I don't want to. To doubt all that Raphaël's death has revealed to me would be to doubt the wild extravagance of life itself. I know now that as long as I can honour, celebrate, protect and engage in that life, I must. Because the Wild and my new sense of the numinous have taught me more than I ever knew, or could imagine knowing, before my kairos moment struck.

Perhaps it's what Icarus knew, as he fell from the sky.

All of it is richer. All of it is stranger.

All of it matters.

EPILOGUE

Three and a half years since Raphaël died, I'm back in France, walking barefoot on the long triangle of land that he rewilded. He's with me in the way he always is, but alongside us is a new companion: my little dog Mishka, whose white fur is already dotted with tiny goosegrass burrs. Still a puppy, she bumbles through the long grass, chasing butterflies, stopping to sniff a new smell, gnaw at a stick, investigate animal droppings, or burrow into a molehill until her face is caked with earth. A world away from the city, we're surrounded by ragwort, gorse, Michaelmas daisies, spider orchids, poppies, cow-parsley and vast tangles of blackberry bushes, their red fruits tight and hard. The pleasure of feeling the dew-drenched grass and soil on my bare skin, to smell the scents of fresh wild mint and thyme, and to see more insects and hear fresh bird-calls than I have in many years is deep and visceral. A few nights ago I heard a nightingale, and every day a pair of grey redstarts visits our veranda. Yesterday, a hare bounded through the long grass, and in the nearby woods I find the eggshells cast off by hatchlings. A birder friend who stayed earlier in the summer tells me that in addition to the blackbirds, carrion crows, robins, woodpigeons, swifts, starlings, sparrows, collared doves, magpies and great tits that we most regularly see, he spotted nuthatch, serin, cirl bunting, house martin, firecrest, blue tit, long-tailed tit, chiffchaff, greenfinch, chaffinch, blackcap, goldfinch, Western Bonelli's warbler, great spotted woodpecker, pied wagtail, jay, and heard golden oriel, cuckoo, raven, jackdaw, turtle dove, melodious warbler, woodlark and tawny owl.

In the distance, by the house, Carsten is working on his novel and Matti and Piluca – now married – are sunning themselves and resting, aware that the next three months are a time to shore up their energy. They will be needing it: in early winter, their twin babies will be born. The pregnancy came easily and unassisted, and with no history of twins in either family, the double blessing feels cornucopian. Raphaël would have loved to be an uncle. But I know that in his way – especially in places that he loved, observed and nurtured, like this patch of vigorously regenerating land – he will be.

I can't know what he'd be doing now if he were still alive. But I know that it would involve activism, in an era in which in many countries public protest has become much harder. The British conservative government's Public Order Act drastically limits the scope of public demonstrations, and emboldened judges are meting out brutally long custodial sentences to frighten those who draw attention to the omni-crisis caused by extractivism, ecocide and climate injustice into silence.

Last summer, the trial of the XR activists accused alongside Raphaël of vandalising the Brazilian Embassy presented his defence to the judge alongside their own statements, and received four-month suspended sentences. Since then, countless other activists all over the world – people who will one day be seen as heroes – have been fined, jailed or murdered for doing what they could to avert catastrophe, concentrations of CO_2 have reached their highest in two million years, the planet has reached its highest temperature in human history, the UN has declared that climate change is 'out of control', and Sir David Attenborough, in his final, iconic 'witness statement', has concluded that 'our blind assault of the planet has finally come to alter the very fundamentals of the living world'. By the time you read this El Niño will have exacerbated global heating and left a slew of disasters in its wake, and there will have been further, even more urgent calls for world leaders, corporations and sections of the media to stop their criminal negligence and step up. While a million species hurtle towards extinction, every year will see increasingly devastating fires, storms, hurricanes and droughts. In the hottest regions of the world, the soaring wet-bulb temperatures that are already causing untold numbers to die of organ failure will take further, devastating tolls on human life. And as the financialisation of the non-human world continues unabated – be it in the form of poaching, trafficking or the mass-scale intensive farming of birds, mammals and even octopuses, new zoonotic pandemics are waiting in the wings. Further symptoms of this turbulent kairos era – among them global recession, the rise of authoritarianism and social extremism, resource wars, soaring poverty and rampant inequality – mean that only the most privileged or wilfully blinkered people can imagine a better future in the immediate term – not for humanity, but for their own descendants. It's no wonder there is a mental health crisis among the young.

This is the world that my grand-daughters will grow up in, and which will form their baseline. Never in human history have new generations been more imperilled than they are now. But my hope for them is active, because in times of reckoning, anxiety, trauma and grief are just part of the story. With every crisis – and this is without doubt the biggest and most fully global one that humans have ever faced – comes an opportunity for fundamental and regenerative change. Our task as a species is to effect this change and avert the worst impacts, if the ten billion people predicted to live on this planet by the end of the century – among them my grand-daughters – are to have the kind of future that Raphaël knew was possible. It's a challenge on a cosmic scale. But it's in our grasp.

The neoliberal status quo that brought us to this point believes the solution is not scaling down consumption but promoting economic growth; the energy companies that spend mind-bending sums distorting and downplaying the evidence of climate science for the sake of profit want us to believe it's the continuation of unlimited access to fossil fuels; some billionaires want us to believe it's through the colonisation of an unhospitable planet.

They're wrong.

A flourishing future involves not more of the same, but visionary ecological change, and the intelligent, committed effort that comes with it. The Covid pandemic showed what vast changes governments and citizens were capable of making at short notice, at a cost that dwarfs what is needed for the world to transition to renewable energy. It means those in power abandoning the wishful thinking that has led us to the brink, and ensuring that the practical steps that can save civilisation from collapse – replacing fossil fuels with renewables, transitioning to a plant-based diet, and living justly and sustainably – are scaled up, speeded up, and addressed with the same urgency as Covid. As individuals, it requires us to see ourselves as citizens rather than consumers, to waste less food and energy, and to travel less, and better. But far more than that, it demands a psychic shift: to acknowledge our grief over all that we are losing, and undergo the regenerative sea-change which brings with it an acceptance that the living world is radically important. Imagine self-interest morphing into common interest, ruthlessness becoming compassion, and injustice being seen – universally – as the basic inhumanity it is. Imagine seeing the natural world not as a human birthright but as a sacred gift, and cherishing the diversity of all the other beings with which we share the planet. Human civilisation is being tested as never before. But there is still time – just – to avert collapse and begin creating the kind of world that future generations can thank us for.

The transformation that leads to the future that Raphaël envisioned, and that billions of others yearn for, is not just urgently necessary. It's an exquisite opportunity. And it's possible.

May we rise to the occasion.

ACKNOWLEDGEMENTS

I'm grateful to my agents Clare Alexander and Lesley Thorne for believing in this book from the start; to Gillian Stern for her inspired insights; to my editor Helena Gonda for her thoughtful and perceptive guidance; to Simon Bramwell for his big, wild heart; to Zoë Blacker for discussing kairos with me; to Morten Kringelbach for conversations about trauma and consciousness; to Kirk Jones for his kindness, generosity and practical help; to Jenny Thomas for putting her own loss to the service of others; to the medium Kat Baillie for channelling Raphaël; to Iain Cameron for his wizardly work on the two websites dedicated to Raphaël's memory and to Cardiac Risk in the Young, The Compassionate Friends, Helping Parents

Heal, Mistet Barn and Det Nationale Sorgcenter for their inspirational help to families in grief.

I thank my elephants, who held me when I needed holding, sat with my silence when I couldn't talk, made space for my pain, shared lessons from their own grief, and took over when I couldn't function. They are the elephants who recommended books, or joined me on walks, the elephants who sent me clips and made films, or read my manuscript in different versions, or were there for me, night or day, to support me through the crucial phases of the first year, and the seasons beyond, reminding me what friendship is for. I am forever indebted to Humphrey Hawksley, Polly Coles, Sandy Gibson, Dorte Bille Harding, Gina de Ferrer, Jane Thynne, Harriet Coles, Sue Brask, Tracey Morton, Amy Kaitlin, Kate O'Riordan, Jojo Wright, Claire Letemendia, Roc Sandford, Annette Lindegaard, Henrik Eriksen, Ebbe Mørk, Charlotte Rørth, Wyl Menmuir, Najieb Khada, Karima Bouylud, Thomas Vinterberg, Pia Jønsson, Eva-Marie Albertsen, Rita Tisdall, Anne Tholstrup, Hanne-Vibeke Holst, Solvej Balle, Simon Lewis, Rea Leman, Randi Nordahl, Stephanie Parker, Collette Havsteen-Mikkelsen, Michael Booth, Helene Neveu-Kringelbach, Mai Misfeldt, Helle Amojne-Marsan, Annabel Markova, Jane Dorner, Laline Paull, Victoria Southgate, Tom Canning and my unstoppable friends and fellow-activists Chloe Aridjis, Toby Litt, Monique Roffey,

James Miller, Jessica Townsend, Paul Ewen, Sharon Eckman, Alex Lockwood and Natasha Walter at Writers Rebel.

To Kira Schrammar, Savannah Sandford, Lazer Sandford, Blue Sandford, Amy Caitlin, Danae Ave, Will Franks, Zappi Taylor, Blythe Pepino, Maya Sherwin, Stephanie Aylett, Femi Agbetuyi, Andre Small, Henry Barclay, Alaia White, Pierre Flasse, Joanna Clark, Saskia Zaig, Yusuf Eesah, Archie Ezekiel, and all of Raphaël's other beloved friends who I don't know but whose names belong here too, I say thank you for lighting up Raphaël's life, for giving him such joy, and for helping him become Iggy Fox.

He loved you all so much.

To my elephant family: Matti Coleman; Pilar Rubio; Las (formerly Laura) Dyhrcrone; Eva Birgitte Jensen; Tom, Sally and Harvey Jensen; Lydia Affie; Anna Kawadji; Karen Wilson; Adam Corcos; and Jenia Levitan, I say thank you for reminding me about the power and constancy of love. And Carsten, fellow-writer and soulmate: since the turn of the century you have been at my side through the best and the worst of times. And every day you have reminded me how good it is to be alive on this Earth, and in this time.

Finally, Raphaël. Thank you for being alive.

Then, now, and always.

PERMISSION CREDITS